'MAKE SENSE WHO MAY'
ESSAYS ON SAMUEL BECKETT'S LATER WORKS

IRISH LITERARY STUDIES

1 *Place, Personality & the Irish Writer*. Andrew Carpenter (editor)
2 *Yeats and Magic*. Mary Catherine Flannery
3 *A Study of the Novels of George Moore*. Richard Allen Cave
4 *J. M. Synge & the Western Mind*. Weldon Thornton
5 *Irish Poetry from Moore to Yeats*. Robert Welch
6 *Yeats, Sligo and Ireland*. A. Norman Jeffares (editor)
7 *Sean O'Casey, Centenary Essays*. David Krause & Robert G. Lowery (editors)
8 *Denis Johnston: A Retrospective*. Joseph Ronsley (editor)
9 *Literature and the Changing Ireland*. Peter Connolly (editor)
10 *James Joyce, An International Perspective*. Suheil Badi Bushrui & Bernard Benstock (editors)
11 *Synge, the Medieval and the Grotesque*. Toni O'Brien Johnson
12 *Carleton's* Traits & Stories *& the 19th Century Anglo-Irish Tradition*. Barbara Hayley
13 *Lady Gregory, Fifty Years After*. Ann Saddlemyer & Colin Smythe (editors)
14 *Woman in Irish Legend, Life and Literature*. S. F. Gallagher (editor)
15 *'Since O'Casey', & Other Essays on Irish Drama*. Robert Hogan
16 *George Moore in Perspective*. Janet Egleson Dunleavy (editor)
17 *W. B. Yeats, Dramatist of Vision*. A. S. Knowland
18 *The Irish Writer and the City*. Maurice Harmon (editor)
19 *O'Casey the Dramatist*. Heinz Kosok
20 *The Double Perspective of Yeats's Aesthetic*. Okifumi Komesu
21 *The Pioneers of Anglo-Irish Fiction 1800-1850*. Barry Sloan
22 *Irish Writers and Society at Large*. Masaru Sekine (editor)
23 *Irish Writers and the Theatre*. Masaru Sekine (editor)
24 *A History of Verse Translation from the Irish, 1789-1897*. Robert Welch
25 *Kate O'Brien: A Literary Portrait*. Lorna Reynolds
26 *Portraying the Self: Sean O'Casey & The Art of Autobiography*. Michael Kenneally
27 *W. B. Yeats and the Tribes of Danu*. P. Alderson Smith
28 *Theatre of Shadows: from* All that Fall *to* Footfalls: *Samuel Beckett's Drama 1956-76*. Rosemary Pountney
29 *Critical Approaches to Anglo-Irish Literature*. Michael Allen & Angela Wilcox (editors)
30 *'Make Sense Who May': Essays on Samuel Beckett's Later Works* Robin J. Davis & Lance St. J. Butler (editors)

‘MAKE SENSE WHO MAY’

ESSAYS ON SAMUEL BECKETT’S LATER WORKS

edited by
Robin J. Davis and Lance St. J. Butler

Irish Literary Studies 30

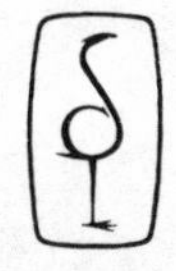

COLIN SMYTHE
Gerrards Cross, 1988

First published in 1988 by Colin Smythe Limited,
Gerrards Cross, Buckinghamshire

British Library Cataloguing in Publication Data
'Make sense who may' : essays on Samuel
Beckett's later works.—(Irish literary
studies; 30).
1. Beckett, Samuel—Criticism and
interpretation
I. Davis, Robin J. II. Butler, Lance
St. John III. Series
822'.912 PR6003.E282Z/

ISBN 0-86140-286-3

Produced in Great Britain
Typeset by Textflow Services Ltd., Belfast, N. Ireland
and printed and bound by Billing & Sons Ltd., Worcester

CONTENTS

INTRODUCTION

Samuel Beckett continues to produce works which challenge our literary and dramatic experience by their unusual forms, their tautness and relative brevity, their sense of music and the visual. He continues to experiment in a wide variety of genres—poetry and prose, drama for radio, television and the stage. He still writes both in English and in French, translating from one into the other, and seeing his work translated into many more languages. His work attracts people who find these different aspects interesting as well as those fascinated by his work as a whole, and this volume is an example of the wide range of approaches sometimes taken by those writing on Beckett.

Eleven of Beckett's works are scrutinised; two radio plays, one television mime, a prose work, and seven works written for the theatre. Most of these were first published or performed in the last ten or fifteen years, but some attention is given to one or two from some years earlier. *Rough for Radio II*, for instance, written in the late sixties, is compared with *All That Fall* (1957), Beckett's first radio play, in an examination of a particular image, that of birth. The television play *Quad* (1982) is situated in the context of Beckett's writing as a whole and revealed as yet another metaphor of questioning and waiting. How many others have dared write a mime for television? Some plays give rise to many questions, controversy even. Does *Catastrophe* (1982), for example, have a political message? Two contrasting views on this are given here, with a third essay written by a linguistic analyst. Men dominate in this play.

The roles for women in such plays as *Not I* (1972), *Footfalls* (1976) and *Rockaby* (1980) are discussed by another contributor with the theory that these plays were written with one actress—Billie Whitelaw—in mind. Several other contributors also tackle these plays, looking at the various questions of ritual and rhythm, language and theatre semiotics, audience response, and the art of the soliloquy itself, so often practiced by Beckett in his dramatic writing. A producer looks at *That Time* (1975) and expounds his own theory of the meaning and relationship of the various sections that make up that extraordinary work. *Ohio impromptu* (1981) also seems to defy all the dramatic conventions: what is it that makes it work in the theatre? An essay on speech act theory attempts to elucidate this mystery. That Beckett takes infinite pains in writing is demonstrated by a close study of the various manuscript drafts that preceded the publication of the short piece we know as *Come and go* (1967). *Ill Seen Ill Said* (1982), is the subject of an essay on irony, with interesting parallels shown with Mallarmé and the symbolist writers. It is the only work of those studied here not written expressly for performance.

It was however given a fine dramatic reading by Angela Pleasence and Sean Barrett at the conference 'Samuel Beckett at eighty' at Stirling University in August 1986. This conference brought together actors and producers, students and scholars, from fifteen countries both Eastern and Western, with plays and exhibitions—and seminars. A considerable number of the papers given at these seminars dealt with Beckett's more recent work, and the present volume gives a selection of these, chosen deliberately to show the different types of criticism his work provokes.

That this selection appears in the present series is thanks, initially at least, to our friend Professor A. Norman Jeffares; it also owes much to the encouragement of our publisher, Colin Smythe. The editors are grateful for their support, and for the collaboration of the fifteen contributors.

Robin J Davis
Lance St. J Butler
Stirling

December 1987

ACKNOWLEDGMENTS

The extracts from *All That Fall, Beckett, Breath, Cascando, Catastrophe, Come and Go, Eh Joe, Endgame, Footfalls, Happy Days, Not I, Ohio Impromptu, A Piece of Monologue, Play, Quad Pieces, Rockaby, Rough for Radio II, That Time, Waiting for Godot* and *What Where* are reproduced here by permission of Faber & Faber Limited.

The extracts from *Dante . . . Bruno . Vico . . Joyce, Ill Seen Ill Said, Malone Dies, Molloy, Murphy, Proust, The Unnameable, Watt,* and *Worstward Ho* are reproduced here by permission of John Calder (Publishers) Ltd.

THE DIFFICULT BIRTH: AN IMAGE OF UTTERANCE IN BECKETT

PAUL LAWLEY

'Astride of a grave and a difficult birth.'[1] The sentence from *Waiting for Godot* provides only the most familiar variant of an image the importance of which has, I think, yet to be fully registered by commentators on Beckett's work. Thanks largely to an emphasis granted by Deidre Bair's account[2] of Beckett's attendance at C. G. Jung's Tavistock lectures in the Autumn of 1935 (the apparent source—if that is the right word—of the figure) and by Walter D. Asmus's account[3] of Beckett's directorial comments on May in *Footfalls*, the critic can approach the image of the 'difficult birth', of a birth imperfect, obstructed or continuing, with an increased confidence in its importance as a (recurrent) means by which Beckett seeks to articulate his sense of 'how it is' with human Being.

In this paper I shall examine the significance of the 'difficult birth' image in two radio plays, and suggest the structural implications for both plays of its pivotal role. I turn first to the sketch written in French in the early 1960's but withheld until it was printed under the title *Pochade Radiophonique* in 1975 and subsequently broadcast in English in 1976 as *Rough for Radio*.[4] This is the piece in which a figure called Fox is coerced into speaking by an Animator and his Stenographer, an added element of persuasion (*rough* as in the punning title) being a bull's-pizzle whip wielded by a mute character called Dick. Martin Esslin, who directed the first broadcast of the piece, tells us that Beckett himself 'regards the work as unfinished, no more than a rough sketch, and felt, having heard the production, that it had "not come off"'. Nevertheless one can agree with Esslin that 'the very roughness of the work gives it its special importance: although it may be more schematic, less refined, by dint of that very circumstance, by representing an early stage of the creative process, it allows us to see structures and methods of Beckett's technique with greater clarity'.[5] It is fitting that the piece should be, as Esslin notes, 'about the artistic process'[6] itself.

The coerced figure in *Rough for Radio II*, Fox, has three utterances.

The most important of these is the third, which precipitates the play's crisis:

—fatigue, what fatigue, my brother inside me, my old twin, ah to be he and he—but no, no no. (*Pause.*) No no. (*Silence. Ruler.*) Me get up, me go on, what a hope, it was he, for hunger. Have yourself opened, Maud would say, opened up, it's nothing, I'll give him suck if he's still alive, ah but no, no no. (*Pause.*) No no. (p. 279)

The image of the male pregnant with his own twin,[7] refusing Caesarian section, is a bizarre one ('it's quite simply impossible!' remarks a scandalized Stenographer (p. 280)), but by virtue of its very explicitness it serves as a focus for Fox's other major utterances. Firstly the one recalled as 'yesterday's close' (p. 276) and read out by the Stenographer:

When I had done soaping the mole, thoroughly rinsing and drying before the embers, what next only out again in the blizzard and put him back in his chamber with his weight of grubs, at that instance his little heart was beating still I swear, ah my God, my God. (*She strikes with her pencil on her desk.*) My God. (p. 277)[8]

Though this image centres on an insertion ('back in his chamber') where the previous one speculates on extraction ('[h]ave yourself opened'), the passages significantly share details involving enclosure (underlined in the case of the 'chamber' by the contrast with the 'blizzard' outside), continuing life ('if he's *still* alive' and 'his little heart was beating *still* I swear') and nourishment ('I'll give him suck' and the 'weight of grubs'). These similarities between the first and last of Fox's utterances provide a context within which the imagery of the second of them takes on a particular suggestiveness:

That for sure, no further, and there gaze, all the way up, all the way down, slow gaze, age upon age, up again, down again, little lichens of my own span, living dead in the stones, and there took to the tunnels. (*Silence. Ruler.*) Oceans too, that too, no denying, I drew near down the tunnels, blue above, blue ahead, that for sure, and there too, no further, ways end, all ends and farewell, farewell and fall, farewell seasons, till I fare again. (*Silence. Ruler.*) Farewell. (p. 279)[9]

If the two passages quoted previously have given us (in turn) a blocked birth and an insertion into a womblike 'chamber', this third one gives us the process of being born itself, a taking to the 'tunnels' for the 'blue' of freedom. Fox speaks here not of facilitating birth or of giving birth but of attempting, apparently in vain ('no further, ways end'), to be born. Or rather, to combine the instances, of giving birth to *himself* (unreleased, unborn, he is 'living dead in the stones'). The impossibility of the wish is reflected in a *verbal* blockage: 'my brother inside me, my old twin, *ah to be he and he*—but no, no no.' Taken together, Fox's three utterances can be seen to construct a scenario of a self-birth attempted yet blocked.

Fox's utterances clearly counterpoint his own position: he is kept hooded, gagged, blindfolded and with his ears plugged; he is required by the Animator and Stenographer to utter words in a seemingly hopeless search for that formulation which would release them, and so him also, from a mysterious obligation. Only his utterance, it seems, can bring them all properly to birth. Thus he must open up, or be 'opened'. This is the word that confirms the counterpoint between his utterances and the whole process represented by the play. 'Having yourself opened, Maud would say, opened up': Fox's phrasing recalls the radio play *Cascando* (1962/3), which is contemporary with*Rough for Radio II* and which has a very similar formal scheme—though the dramatic situation is much more abstract in presentation. Here a controller seeks to extract a definitive ending from a Voice and Music; this controller is called the 'Opener' after his function:

I'm afraid to open.
But I must open
So I open.[10]

In the light, then, of *Cascando* (*Rough's* 'old twin'?), Fox's '[h]ave yourself opened' can be seen to combine the ideas of forced birth and forced utterance: utterance has gathered an ontological significance.

We can take the first step in the definition of that significance by considering the animal and animal-related references in the play. 'Fox surely equals *Vox*',[11] remarks Martin Esslin, yet the fox itself is worth bearing in mind when we also hear of the mole that Fox 'soaped' and '[v]ermin in the lingerie' (p. 275)[12] of the Stenographer and of '[t]hose fodient rodents' (p. 282) exclaimed at by the Animator. And when we hear the Animator speaking of the object of their search as a 'sign or *set* of words' (p. 282, my emphasis), we might recognize the punning presence of the badger, which, though not a rodent, is certainly, like all the other creatures mentioned, fodient—that is, a burrower. Fox images himself 'down the tunnels, blue above, blue ahead'. Throughout his creative life Beckett seems to have thought of the artistic process in similar terms. In the third of the *Three Dialogues with Georges Duthuit* (1949) he speaks of the artist's '*warren* of modes and attitudes'[13] (my emphasis), and in *Proust* (1931) he maintains: 'The only fertile research is *excavatory*, immersive, a contraction of the spirit, a descent'[14] (my emphasis). (In the present context, and in close contact with the adjective 'fertile', 'contraction' seems to yield a specific association: 'The artistic tendency is not expansive, but a *contraction*'[15] (my emphasis).)

The importance of these images, in both plays and critical writing, is in their suggestion of artistic creation as a process taking place in the absence of a fixed and definitive position, indeed as a process *obliged* to take place *because* of the absence of a fixed and definitive position. 'Modes and attitudes' are provided, but these are by their very nature provisional, temporary, shifting ('[c]ome, come, sir, don't say that, it is part of your rôle, as animator' (p. 283)). What the process results in is a network, a set of relations rather than a single site. The characteristic creative 'position' is *between* or *through*—a *pre*position rather than a position. The pun which, in the underground linguistic network of *Rough for Radio II*, furnishes the link between burrowing and writing is delivered in the Animator's request to the Stenographer: 'How does the *passage* go again?' (p. 281, my emphasis) 'May we have that passage again, miss?' (p. 284)[16] He is asking for the passage (or extract or section—suddenly these words are playful) about the male pregnant with his 'old twin'—that is, for a passage about the crucial *absence* of passage, at least of passage to freedom.

The play as a whole is concerned with forms of intercourse and blockage. Its action, like that of the other radio plays of the early 1960's, consists of a gradual revelation of the desperate interdependence (under some external obligation) of separate parties whose relationship is initially presented as being of a settled Master/Slave type. The fluidity of identity by which fixed characters are revealed as 'modes and attitudes' is here imaged by the exchange or influence (in both usual and literal senses) of various sorts of bodily fluids. Blood when the Stenographer is ordered to kiss Fox '[t]ill it bleeds! Kiss it white! (*Howl from* Fox.) Suck his gullet!' (p. 282) Semen when the Animator speculates about the Maud mentioned by Fox: 'Someone had fecundated her' (p. 283), (one might also mention the 'bull's pizzle' (p. 275) of the mute persuader, Dick). And, most importantly, milk and tears (which seem to be associated here): Fox speaks of Maud's saying 'I'll give him suck if he's still alive' then weeps (p. 279), and towards the end of the play the Animator, apparently infected by Fox's tears, 'snivels' repeatedly, calls for a handkerchief and is heard to blow his nose 'abundantly' (pp. 281-82). But it is the Stenographer who, in her role as mediatrix, is most liable to pass, through milk and tears, into the world of Fox's discourse. She provides the initial link between that world and her own life by remarking that 'my nanny was a Maud' (p. 280). It is she who kisses Fox so deeply as to reach his very entrails and who is finally, as she quotes his words, this time (as in his own delivery of them) 'tremulous[ly]' (p. 284), flooded and silenced by his tears. The association of the Stenographer with Fox is effected by the Animator's emphatic imputation to Fox of the phrase 'between two kisses', which inserts the Stenographer (and her kissing of Fox) *into* Fox's discourse: 'Have yourself opened, Maud would say, between two kisses, opened up . . .' (p. 284). The detail is a crucial one, for it signals an implicit acceptance of Fox's birth-scenario and within it casts the Stenographer as Maud, midwife and wet-nurse (she '*suck[s]* his gullet' as Maud offers to 'give him *suck*'). That, in a metaphorical sense, is what her role has been throughout the play. But that metaphorical sense is now fast merging into a literal one. Our sense of the separateness of metaphorical and literal levels becomes increasingly confused and the 'real' and 'created' worlds of the play become unstable terms. Fox is obviously *contained* by Animator and Stenographer, but his discourse, which is itself about containment and issuing forth, seems in turn to contain (by representing) the ontological position of all three figures. We are momentarily in doubt as to who is *inside* what or whom: '[M]y brother inside me . . . ah to be he and he—'

At the close of the play, then, the world of Animator and Stenographer seems to be flowing into that of Fox's discourse. In such circumstances, weeping, lactation and fecundation serve to articulate the passage between one created mode and another:

A: Well . . . you know . . . I may be wrong . . . I wouldn't like to . . . I hardly dare say it . . . but it seems to me that . . . here . . . possibly . . . we have something at last.
S: Would to God, sir.
A: Particularly with that tear so hard behind. It is not the first, agreed. But in such a context!
S: And the milk, sir, don't forget the milk.
A: The breast! One can almost see it!
S: Who got her in that condition, there's another question for us.
A: What condition, miss, I fail to follow you.
S: Someone has fecundated her. (*Pause. Impatient.*) If she is in milk someone must have fecundated her.
A: To be sure!

S: Who?
A: (*Very excited.*) You mean . . .
S: I ask myself.
(pp. 283-84)

They seem near to (a) solution, yet the fluidity of identity at the end of the play brings not the wished-for freedom, a birth into genuine being, but only a *displacement* of relations and tensions. The blockage remains, the vital passage is unopened, though '[t]omorrow, who knows, we may be free' (p. 284).[17]

The figural world of *Rough for Radio II* is one of burrowing and passage and recurrent blockage. That of the earlier *All That Fall* (1956)[18] seems very different, yet a version of the 'warren of modes and attitudes' is apparent here too. Its relation to the medium itself is focussed in a pair of puns. When Mrs Rooney says (with some passion) to Mr Barrell, '[w]e all know your station is the best kept of the entire network, but there are times when that is not enough, just not enough' (pp. 186-87), we may reflect, as radio listeners, that rail systems are not the only ones that have *stations* and *networks*. The 'warren' in this instance is the network, and the stations—in the broadest sense, the stationary points—are 'just not enough' because they can, it seems, only ever be 'modes and attitudes'—provisional and temporary. 'No other play by Beckett', says Clas Zilliacus, 'relies to the extent that *All That Fall* does on motion in space'. [19] Beckett's initial idea for the play had to do with modes of locomotion. In a letter he told Nancy Cunard: 'Never thought about a radio play technique, but in the dead of t'other night got a nice gruesome idea full of cartwheels and dragging feet and puffing and panting which may or may not lead to something'[20] (and how characteristic the merging of author's task with characters' efforts in 'lead to something'!). But, as Hugh Kenner argues: 'All these movements in space are translated by the aural medium into time, where sounds expend themselves and die. . . . Thus the mode in which the play itself exists, as a series of auditory effects in time, sustains its theme of transience.'[21] Brief stationary moments on the journey are taken as opportunities for the striking of verbal attitudes: 'Let us halt a moment and let this vile dust fall back upon the viler worms' (p. 175). 'What are we standing here for? This dust will not settle in our time' (p. 176). All the same, stasis here is a void, not a plenitude of being. They must have the sounds of travelling: 'Stand her up, I beseech you, and let us be off. This is awful!' (p. 178). Their true haven would be reached only by way of the 'other roads, in other lands' that Dan dreams of; it is 'another home' (both p. 192), different from the one they are making for. In *All That Fall* the stationary/moving opposition is deconstructed by the medium itself.

We must bear this in mind as we move to consider the birth-idea in the play, for it is articulated largely in terms of stasis and movement. Of course, as every listener and critic has noted, the idea is clearly and comically (if not subtly) present in Maddy's issuing forth from Mr Slocum's car (on pp. 179-80, after their uproarious congress as she mounts up into it on p. 178). I want to focus, however, on Dan's arrival at Boghill station and on his narrative about the journey, together with Maddy's response.

Having asserted that the train 'drew out on the tick of time' (p. 192) and that he was '[a]lone in the compartment' (p. 193), Dan describes how he worked out that by retiring he 'would add very considerably' to his income. But he goes on to tell how he reflected on the 'horrors of home life', which are evoked in terms of process: '[T]he dusting, sweeping, airing, scrubbing, waxing, waning', etc. The energetic list comes to a climax with the thought of 'the happy little healthy little howling neighbours' brats' (all p. 193). With these prospective horrors he contrasts his 'silent, backstreet, basement office' (p. 193). With its 'rest-couch and velvet hangings' (pp. 193-94) the office seems womblike, but a wombtomb, a womb *after* life rather than before. The name-plate, once a sign of identity, is 'obliterated' (p. 193) and Dan muses on being 'buried there alive': 'Nothing, I said, not even fully certified death, can ever take the place of that' (p. 194). The office is like a womb in that it encloses life and like a tomb in that the state seems terminal. (Compare with this Fox's 'living dead in the stones' in *Rough for Radio II*.)

A counterpoint is meanwhile being set up within the story itself. Dan argues the pros and cons of retirement 'to the lilt of the bogeys' (p. 193) as he travels. However, as he recalls considering his office and being 'buried there alive', he remarks: 'It was then I noticed that we were at a standstill' (p. 194). This is an important detail, as it signals a shift of narrative level within the story. The illusory, temporary nature of Dan's ideal mode of existence is revealed not in his recollection of his thoughts about business, but in his account of what happened on the journey. His backstreet office and the contentment he feels at the limbo it provides him with is displaced to or reproduced in the compartment of the static train. Even when he realised '[w]e had not entered a station', he says, 'I just sat on, saying, If this train were never to move again I should not greatly mind', But:

Then gradually a—how shall I say—a growing desire to—er—you know—welled up within me. Nervous probably. In fact now I am sure. You know, the feeling of being confined. (p. 195)

To paraphrase this as an account of bladder trouble due to claustrophobia would be to miss its suggestive points altogether. First of all there is the problem of utterance ('how shall I say'). On the literal level, of course, this is merely a matter of social delicacy ('er'), but followed as it is by figures of containment within('welled up within me') and of *being* contained ('the feeling of being confined'), it offers another inflection of meaning. 'Confined' is the key word, for the person who both confines and is confined (*in confinement*) is the bearer of a child ('[y]es yes, I have been through that', comments Maddy on Dan's feeling). I say 'person' because here again the case pertains to the male. Dan is giving himself birth. 'Where was I in my composition?' (p. 194) he asks Maddy: the pun is vital, for the making up (?) of his narrative is also a *self-production*, both in its function and in the process it describes. Reading in this way, we may suggest that the narrative is a 'composition' not because it may be telling lies or excluding facts from a set of events fixed in the past but because it seeks to construct a substantial present through language.

In his compartment, Dan paces 'to and fro between the seats, like a caged beast' (one of several hints at his potential for a child-killing savagery in his pent state). 'After what seemed an eternity' the train moves off, and the arrival, with Dan's mysteriously delayed issuing forth, involves a naming—'the next thing was Barrell bawling the abhorred name' (we recall the 'obliterated plate' of the office)—and a kind of sexing—'I got down and Jerry led me to the men's' (all p. 195). This is the point at which the listening audience 'comes in' and can begin hearing for itself. If an underlying birth-scenario seems far-fetched, we might consider Maddy's cries, at the climax of the station-scene: 'The up mail! The up mail!' (a pun evident earlier in the play)—together with Tommy's cry: 'She's coming'—and, on the arrival of the down train, the direction (thoroughly in the spirit of the one in *Happy Days* which describes Willie as 'dressed to kill'[22]) '*clashing of couplings*' (all p. 187). When Dan finally emerges from 'the men's' Maddy tells him that it is his birthday (p. 188).

It might fairly be argued that in reading Dan's journey and arrival as a birth-scenario I am forcing undue specificity upon a pattern which is indeed apparent in this part of the play—that of confinement and release. However if we do accept the birth-scenario we are in a position to interpret Maddy's recollection after Dan's 'composition', which on the face of it has no connection whatever with anything he has said, as a *displaced* response to his request, 'Maddy. Say you believe me' (p. 195).

Maddy remembers 'once attending a lecture by one of these new mind doctors' who told 'the story of a little girl, very strange and unhappy in her ways'. Treatment was unsuccessful and he 'was finally obliged to give up the case. . . . The only thing wrong with her as far as he could see was that she was dying' (pp. 195-96). But Maddy has been haunted ever since the lecture by 'something he said, and the way he said it':

> When he had done with the little girl he stood there motionless for some time, quite two minutes I should say, looking down at his table. Then he suddenly raised his head and exclaimed, as if he had had a revelation, The trouble with her was she had never really been born! (p. 196)

'There is nothing to be done for those people!' (p. 196), Maddy exclaims, yet despite the effort to distinguish them from us, 'those people' are *ALL* That Fall, *all* mortals. The revelatory moment (for Maddy if not necessarily for the lecturer himself) is brought about by one who, unlike the people of the play, can *afford* motionlessness and who is suddenly able to raise his head amidst all the world's falling. For Maddy the 'mind doctor' is momentarily outside the common process. Her recollection is a response to Dan's attempt to compose himself, to formulate a birth-scenario for himself. The very need for such self-composition hints at the general truth of the lecturer's particular 'diagnosis': 'The trouble with her was she had never really been born!' That sentence is a pivotal moment not just in this play but, I would contend, in Beckett's work as a whole.

In the course of some interesting paragraphs on Dan's 'composition' and Maddy's response, Charles R. Lyons comments: 'Rooney's recitation of his passage on the train, which omits the central incident, is answered by another recitation which reports the strange death of a young girl.'[23] The central incident is of course the death, reported by the boy Jerry, of the little child that fell from the train '[o]n to the line . . . Under the wheels' (p. 199), the incident that causes the late arrival of the train. There are several hints, noticed by all critics, of Dan's child-killing potential.[24] Taken together, these strongly suggest that Dan wants Maddy to believe his story because it is a fabrication designed to conceal from her his act of murder. However I am not sure that this central incident is *simply* omitted. Falling is the play's figure for dying, and dying, in Maddy's story of the little girl, is expressed as a state of 'never really [having] been born' ('[t]he only thing wrong with her . . . was that she was dying'). The '*little* child' (p. 199, my emphasis) that falls from the train surely echoes powerfully the '*little* girl' who had never really been born—just as they both echo Maddy's dead child '[l]ittle Minnie' (p. 174) and are gathered up in 'Death and the Maiden' (p. 197; also p. 172). I think we have here another variant of the *Godot* image: 'Astride of a grave and a difficult birth.' The child is being given 'birth to into death'.[25] Her death, like Dan's 'composition' but this time paradoxically, is a birth-scenario. His story does not omit but *counterpoints* what he dare not (for Maddy's sake) mention. If he has a role, it is perhaps that of the gravedigger/obstetrician of the *Godot* image, '[putting] on the forceps'.[26] His business premises, after all, afford him access to both life and death (he is 'buried there alive'), and if his rage is that of one who might bring about death, it does not prevent him from shedding tears when he recognises (as Maddy apparently does not) 'Death and the Maiden', with its grave aptness to the events he is concealing. Between Death and the Maiden he seems to be the mediator.[27]

In identifying and elucidating scenarios of 'difficult birth' in these two plays, I have been concerned speculatively to suggest and to exploit the centrality to both pieces of pun and wordplay. The characteristic density of Beckett's verbal medium promotes in the listener a consciousness of the continuous *generation* of the dramatic world. Our sense of the createdness of that world involves us in the dynamic of process which is so energetically evoked and abhorred by Dan Rooney. (And we are never more conscious of this createdness than at the moment of incipient collapse dramatised in *Rough for Radio II*.) The connection between the figure of the 'difficult birth' and the generation of the dramatic world is, I would contend, more than merely fortuitous. The figure penetrates the dramatic medium, or, perhaps, better, the medium *informs* the figure, for in the 'difficult birth' Beckett has found a figure within which the energies of his perennial preoccupations—imperfect being, utterance and the process of creation—are simultaneously contained and released.[28]

The words falling from his mouth. Making do with his mouth. Lights lamp as described. Backs away to edge of light and turns to face wall. Stares beyond into dark. Waits for first word always the same. It gathers in his mouth. Parts lips and thrusts tongue forward. Birth.[29]

LESS = MORE: DEVELOPING AMBIGUITY IN THE DRAFTS OF *COME AND GO*

ROSEMARY POUNTNEY

The version of *Come and Go* bearing the least relation to the published text is a typescript at Reading University Library headed 'Scene 1'. Its title suggests that it is the first scene of a sketch. Since the scene stands very much alone in the play's development, we will consider it first. There are three characters, Viola, Poppy and Rose. Poppy reads aloud from a titillating book, interrupted at intervals by the others. Viola asks her to re-read an earlier passage, in order to establish the whereabouts of the romantic hero, Aubrey, whose habits recall those of Willie in *Happy Days*:

Poppy '. . . Aubrey stretched out to the flames his long hairy legs, took a sip of his ~~brandy~~ *Sandeman* relit his cigar and resumed alone his collection of obscene postcards.'[1]

Literal-minded Viola, having established Aubrey's current occupation, is not prepared to hear more until she has ascertained the level of his trousers:

Viola Are his trousers off already then?
Rose Not in my recollection—why?
Viola His long hairy legs.
Rose ~~A lover's~~ *The* legs may be hairy and ~~his~~ *the* trousers still *be* on. Poppy.
Poppy (who has been checking the text) When last seen his trousers were still on.

Poppy continues reading, a parody of pornographic writing that arouses Viola's critical faculties:

Poppy '. . . then falling to her knees plunged them between her thighs in an ecstasy of anticipation.'
Viola This is ~~careless~~ *slipshod* writing.
Rose You mean one cannot plunge one's knees between one's thighs?

The sketch ends with Poppy, apparently overcome by her text, leaving the room:

Poppy '. . . Finally she sprang to her feet and, still moist, entered the ~~darkened~~ bedroom.' Excuse me just one moment.
Poppy gets up, lays down the book and goes out laboriously.

I have quoted liberally from this typescript to indicate how little connects its hilarious revue-like style with the disturbing short text that is finally printed. Beckett must have realised its inappropriateness as a first scene and the entire script is crossed out in his hand.

In a holograph also at Reading University, and headed by Beckett 'Before *Come and Go*', there are two separate attempts at a text much nearer the final version. The first of these is headed *Good Heavens* and the second *Type of Confidence*. It appears, however, that the latter is the first attempt and *Good Heavens* a rewrite, although Beckett has headed *Good Heavens* 'Before *Come and Go*, as though it were the earlier version. But a comparison between the vocabulary of the two texts shows *Good Heavens* improving upon that of *Type of Confidence*: 'No!' says B (appalled) in *Type of Confidence*—but in the second text 'No!' is crossed out in favour of 'Good heavens!'. Moreover A in *Type of Confidence* (the women are nameless in both texts and differentiated only alphabetically), says: '. . .She thinks it is acidity' but in *Good Heavens* 'acidity' is altered to 'heartburn'. Furthermore C's sister (who is mentioned in both texts) is nameless in *Type of Confidence*, but becomes 'Mrs. Flower' in *Good Heavens*.

Assuming that the misplacement hypothesis is correct, we can now see that Beckett had plotted the structure of the entire play before writing any dialogue. The *Type of Confidence* heading appears on a clean sheet, as would be expected of a new draft. But, at the top of the sheet, above the title, is the following diagram:

	1 ABC.	
	2 ~~AB~~ *Exit C*	
B knows about C	3 A to B about C ~~B to C~~	A *knows about* C
" " " *A*		A " " B
	4 Enter C.	
	5 Exit A.	
C knows about A		

C knows about B

6 B to C about A ~~C to B~~
7 Enter A.
8 Exit B.
9 C to A about B ~~A to C~~
10 Enter B

Beckett began the play with the structure of three confidential gossips clearly in mind, and after jotting down the structure sketched a 'type' (or illustration) of the kind of confidence he had in mind, before going on to draft the play in full. As would be expected were this the case, *Type of Confidence* is just a fragment, and consists solely of dialogue between A and B, ending on the entrance of C, but *Good Heavens* is almost complete, apart from the final conversation between C and A. In both texts the conversation centres on two secrets: first how each women manages to achieve her apparently flawless complexion and secondly the fact that the absent member of the trio is suffering from terminal illness. Beckett intends from the start (as the diagram shows) that all three women should gossip and be gossiped about. The difference between what is said face to face and what is said behind the back of the missing person reveals both a devastating feminine hypocrisy and the irony that the secret is told by someone whom the hearer already knows (or soon discovers) to be doomed also. And most ironical of all, while each woman muses upon the fate of the other two, she remains supremely unaware of her own. In *Good Heavens*, each expresses admiration for the complexion of that other with whom she is left alone, while silently appalled by how ill she looks. A merciful lie (A says: 'You do look wonderful'; and B: 'You look so fresh') each time succeeds in drawing from the other woman the secret behind her so-called radiant skin. A confesses that her beauty secret is a discharged prisoner, C's is: 'the croquet champion' while B seems to have attended a brothel:

A Good Heavens! Is that place going still?
B Oh very much so. (*Complacent laugh.*) Very much so indeed.

B in fact makes a further self-revelation, capable of even broader interpretation, not to mention a side-swipe at the university:

~~B~~*C* . . . Have you been using something on your skin?
(~~C~~*B*whispers in ~~B~~ *C's* ear.)
~~B~~ Good heavens! ~~Is he up again?~~
B Oh very much so. (*Complacent laugh.*) Very much so indeed!
B No cream to touch it.
~~B~~*C* I did not know he was up.

Alterations in this piece of dialogue show that Beckett at times became confused as to what dialogue belonged to which woman, showing that he was thinking in terms of what had to be said, rather than who should say it. The voices are mouthpieces, letters of the alphabet rather than characters, and Beckett is merely working out the pattern he set himself in the preliminary diagram. Even when names appear the personalities are indistinguishable, as if the three women were one, and indeed the costume note in the published text reads:

> Apart from colour differentiation, three figures as alike as possible. That all three women are aspects of a single personality is of course an attractive explanation for their extraordinary resemblance and mutual mortal illness, but the deliberate ambiguities allow for the possibility that Beckett may simply be developing his perennial theme of birth 'astride of a grave'.

The precise nature of the secret concerning each woman in the published text remains undisclosed. But in the holograph, though also whispered, the secrets are at once clarified for the audience by the recipient's responses. The comic open secrets (the complexion cures) in each gossip are followed by a second secret, that both reminds us of the published text (by the 'appalled' response it elicits) and is unlike it, in that serious illness is not implied, but explicit and fatal:

A. She told me she was condemned.
(*She whispers in B's ear,*)
B. (*Appalled.*) ~~No!~~ *Good heavens!*
A. The worst kind. (*Pause.*) Three months. (*Pause.*) At the outside.

A final typescript at Reading University is also headed 'Before *Come and Go*' in Beckett's hand and is a further attempt to share the conversations taking place between two of the women in the absence of the third. Each gossip is typed on a separate sheet and the women are now named, Rose, Vi and Poppy. This is both an extension of the holograph (in which the only name mentioned was 'Mrs. Flower') and an abbreviation of 'Scene One', which has 'Viola' rather than 'Vi'. In each gossip instead of a mutual exchange of sexual confidences, only one of the women now discloses her complexion recipe, and this is followed by hushed discussion of the imminent demise of the absentee. There is, however, a comic extension of this draft, the introduction of three sorrowing husbands—all conspicuously absent from the marital home:

Rose (of Poppy).	I ran into her husband at the Gaiety. He is half crazed with grief.
Poppy (of Vi).	Her husband wrote me from Madeira. He is heartbroken.
Vi (of Rose).	Her husband called *me* from Naples. He was weeping over the wire.

The final typescript of the 'Before *Come and Go*' drafts at Reading University is classified by the same manuscript number as the comic 'Scene One' we looked at first, thus suggesting it follows on from Scene I, as a second scene, and indeed (apparently supporting this view) the first page is headed II in Roman figures. Since, however, the second page is headed IV and the third VI (also in Roman numerals) it becomes evident that these numbers represent stage II, IV and VI of Beckett's structural plan for the play (i. e. the three gossips). Indeed after the first gossip he sketches in the plan:

I V. R. P.
II V. R.
III V. R. P.
IV P. R.
V V. R. P.
VI V. P.
VII V. R. P.

Stages I, III, V and VII thus consist of the linking material that we find in the published text, before, between and after the gossips, when all three women are present onstage. It is possible that the hilarious 'Scene One' was Beckett's first attempt at drafting such linking material.

The second typescript at Reading University is thus not simply a second scene, nor even a single scene, but scenes 2, 4 and 6, three separate stages in the play's development. Although Beckett could not resist the comic introduction of sorrowing husbands at this stage, he has already begun to cut and shape the play, so that the precise patterning of the final text is beginning to emerge. Except for the structural plan, however (which is handwritten), the entire second typescript is crossed through; but a further note in Beckett's hand, on the back of the last sheet, describes the piece as a 'dramaticule'.

The Manus Presse at Stuttgart published in 1968 facsimiles of two further holographs of *Come and Go*, which reveal a text much nearer its final form than the Reading material. In the first of these Beckett reverts to the ABC characterization of the Reading holographs, but he has begun to work on the linking scenes, as well as restructuring the gossips. By the second Stuttgart facsimile the text as we know it has largely evolved and A becomes Ru, C Vi and B Flo. The last line of this draft is perhaps the most interesting—it reads:

Flo: I can feel ~~your~~ *the* rings.

The advantage of making the reference to rings non-specific and ambiguous has occurred to Beckett here, as we shall see.

The remaining drafts of the play are four typescripts at Washington University, St. Louis; these are largely fair copies, except for the addition in the second of them of a little extra text in Beckett's hand, at the opening and close of the play. At the opening Vi is to speak the name of each of the other women (who both reply 'Yes') in contrast to a telling insertion at the end of the play in which Flo is to speak the names of the other two women (before saying she can feel the rings) but is answered only by silence. These insertions are not present in the Calder and Boyars text of 1967, while the Grove Press version of 1968 (*Cascando and other short dramatic pieces*) incorporates only the additional dialogue at the opening of the play and not the extra words at its close.

In the drafts of *Come and Go* we see Beckett advancing towards an ever stricter patterning, cutting and shaping until, as with a poem, not a word can be lost. By the final text he achieves the effect of repetition through a subtle combination of variations on a theme. The two secrets, for example, are reduced to one. The women's responses all concern God, but are linguistically varied (God grant not/God forbid/ Please God not), invoking respectively a generous, a forbidding and a merciful God. Visually too the direction notes, particularly those on costume and movement, emphasise the theme of similarity with difference. The colours worn are different, but all 'dulled', the faces are all shaded by hats and all three women move noiselessly into and out of the surrounding shadow. Their voices are all specifically required to be 'as low as compatible with audibility' and 'colourless except for three "Ohs" and two lines following'. The sense of ritual in both language and movement is strengthened by the final joining of hands, while the carefully plotted hand positioning seems to embrace the three women in the form of a Celtic 'endless' knot, symbolising infinity.

The beauty of the final version is its brevity: movement stylised, dialogue pared to 121 words, but perfectly patterned and proportioned. The more concise, the more highly stylised Beckett's 'dramaticule' becomes, the more telling it is, until the final point is wordless. 'I can feel the rings', says Flo, as the three women sit, hands linked, staring into space. But it is on three pairs of ringless hands that the light focuses just before the curtain falls. The power and economy of such an ending is the work of a master craftsman. Not until after the last line has been spoken is a further dimension added to the play by the light, which teases the mind into additional speculation. The stage directions state that it is the women's hands rather than their faces which are 'made up to be as visible as possible' and that there are 'no rings apparent'. As soon as this point is registered, the full force of the play begins to emerge and the various hints fall into place. Three lifetimes are suggested in the 121 words of the final Calder text. Three faded flowers sit recalling the days of their freshness 'at Miss Wade's'. Their floral names have been abbreviated to single syllables, their colours are dulled. Ru is in violet—and the puns are intentional. There is nothing left to these women but rue for the love that had passed them by. Gone are the lovers and sorrowing husbands of the early drafts. The only reference to love in the published text is 'Dreaming' and the only sexual experience known to these women appears to have been in fantasy. The play indeed ends in fantasy as Flo asserts she can feel the rings that are not there.

The fact that the women see 'little change' in each other is significant. The overriding impression of the play is of lack of event. Precisely the tragedy of the women in *Come and Go* is that they appear perpetually to have been waiting for an event, possibly marriage, that never happens. And now, with death looming, an unwanted lover in the shade, they seem to be about to die before having ever fully lived; 'never been properly born' as Beckett notes laconically in the Appendix to *Watt*. In the nightmare vision of his later drama the three women may indeed have to endure permanent waiting, condemned to an after-life in which the perpetually active consciousness spends its time endlessly recounting its life. *Come and Go* is the waiting situation in Chekov's *Three Sisters*, or in *Godot*, reduced to its essence. Indeed the play brings a host of literary analogies to mind quite apart from *Macbeth*, to which our attention is directed at the outset. Its brevity makes us forcibly aware of impermanence, that (as in Gray's 'Elegy written in a Country Churchyard' or in *Twelfth Night*) 'Beauty's a flower' and must fade. Death 'the invisible worm' in Blake's poem 'The Sick Rose' is already at work. Looking at the Blake, it seems very likely that Beckett had the analogy in mind when writing *Come and Go*:

O Rose thou art sick.
The invisible worm,
That flies in the night
In the howling storm:

Has found out thy bed
Of crimson joy:
And his dark secret love
Does thy life destroy.[2]

'How do you think Rose is looking?' enquires Poppy in the second Reading University typescript. 'Sick.' replies Vi.

Instead of the tangible lovers of the early drafts and the explicit discussions about mortality, the final text is ambiguous. The probability, given the horror with which each secret is received, is that it is Death (the lover in Matthias Claudius's poem 'Der Tod und das Mädchen) who stretches out his arms to the three women from the surrounding darkness. In the 18th century poem, Death accosts a young girl:

Gib Deine Hand, du schön und zart Gebild:
Bin Freund und komme nicht zu strafen.
Sei gutes Muts! Ich bin nicht wild!
Sollst sanft in meinen Armes schlafen!

[Give me your hand, you lovely tender creature:
I am your friend and haven't come to punish you.
Don't be afraid! I am not cruel!
You will sleep sweetly in my arms.][3]

It was to this poem that Schubert composed his Quartet in D Minor (D810—'Death and the Maiden') that lies at the heart of *All That Fall* and the same poem lies behind Krapp's uneasy glances over his shoulder into the shadows in Beckett's rehearsals of *Krapp's Last Tape*. Beckett describes the action as 'Hain', which he explained to me succinctly as follows:

Freund Hain (or Hein = Heinrich)
= Death (easeful) the Scytheman

and referred me to the Matthias Claudius poem. The poem so haunts Beckett's imagination that it seems likely that it forms part of the experience of *Come and Go* also, a play in which all three characters are clasped in a circle of darkness.

The ambiguities in the final version of *Come and Go* fill out with surprising richness and depth, a textually bare play. Beckett has achieved this effect by combining an obscure minimal text with precise and explicit stage directions, capable of directing audience attention to possibilities not verbally stated and making the play a *tour de force*.

SEEING IS PERCEIVING: BECKETT'S LATER PLAYS AND THE THEORY OF AUDIENCE RESPONSE

KAREN L. LAUGHLIN

Critics have long been aware of Samuel Beckett's insistence on the clarity of his dramatic situations and his refusal to become involved in the exegesis of his plays. '[W]e have no elucidations to offer of mysteries that are all of [the journalists'] making', reads his well-known letter to Alan Schneider. 'My work is a matter of fundamental sounds (no joke intended) made as fully as possible, and I accept responsibility for nothing else. If people want to have headaches among the overtones, let them. And provide their own aspirin.'[1] Bearing this warning in mind, the following essay does not propose yet another interpretation of Beckett's dramatic works but rather explores the complex relationship between Beckett's stage plays and their theatre audiences. Drawing on recent research in the fields of semiotics and reader-oriented criticism, this paper elucidates some of the ways these plays elicit and guide audience participation in the theatrical event of their performance; more specifically, it considers how Beckett's plays move their spectators beyond exegesis into a theatrical experience of a very different sort, one grounded in the theatre's material aspects (its 'fundamental sounds') and in what might be termed the 'polyphonic' nature of their theatrical presentation.[2]

Beckett's later plays provide especially fertile ground for the study of audience response. In their very sparseness and challenges to dramatic conventions, these plays help to 'lay bare' the specific nature of the dramatic work and its implications for their reception.[3] As critics were quick to point out, even Beckett's earliest plays included self-conscious references to their own status as dramatic works. One need only recall Pozzo's grand oratory in *Godot* or Clov's reference to 'making an exit' in *Endgame*[4] to become aware of the self-reflexivity of Beckett's drama. Equally often, this reflection on the dramatic medium points to audience response as part of the explicit conditions of performance. Surely the spectators are meant to share in Vladimir and Estragon's feelings of boredom during the endless wait for Godot and to consider their own position as the 'Mere eye. No mind. Opening and shutting on' M at the end of *Play*[5]. In the later plays, Beckett has continued this pattern. Most obviously, of course, the rehearsal depicted in *Catastrophe* ends with a 'distant storm of applause' which fades as P 'fixes the audience' in his gaze.[6] The hooded Auditor of *Not I* likewise appears as an on-stage double for the theatre spectator while the Woman's Voice of *Footfalls* exhorts the audience, 'let us watch her move, in silence'.[7]

These latter examples already reveal the particular effectiveness of Beckett's plays in laying bare conventions governing play-audience interaction. The Voice of *Footfalls*, for example, reminds us that we generally watch the dramatic spectacle 'in silence', however much we might naively wish to intercede on behalf of the plays' beleaguered protagonists. Similarly, the Auditor's helpless gestures in *Not I* not only signal the presence of someone listening to Mouth's monologue, but also underline the limited scope of audience-to-actor communication.[8] Like the Auditor, we can only offer Mouth—or the actress who must work so hard to portray her—a silent indication of our 'helpless compassion' (Beckett's own description of the Auditor's movements).[9] Mouth herself highlights the asymmetrical relationship between the play and its audience when she speaks of 'straining to hear . . . make something of it . . . not catching the half . . . not the quarter . . . no idea what she's saying'.[10] Since, in performance, Mouth's story is usually recited at break-neck speed, the audience, like the story's protagonist, finds itself straining to catch the spoken words and 'make something' of them.

In its portrayal of the seemingly un-dramatic act of reading, *Ohio Impromptu* offers a contrasting reflection of the play-audience relationship. Once again, we find an on-stage listener, here identified as L, who does not verbally respond to the speaker's onrush of words. But by knocking on the table, L causes R to repeat selected passages of the book he is reading aloud. L's control over the time-flow of the reading, recalling Krapp's earlier relishing in selected passages from his tapes, sets L apart from the theatre spectator, for whom Beckett's plays often continue relentlessly, in spite of our inability to keep up with them.[11]

However, it is not only through self-reflection that Beckett's later plays illuminate the nature of audience response. Both their challenges to many of drama's basic conventions and their peculiar counterpoint of verbal language and scenic detail have important consequences for Beckett's spectator. One of the most striking features of the later plays, for example, is their frequent reliance on narration, or the recounting of off-stage events by figures whose words are not clearly addressed to other characters on stage. Beckett initiated this denial of drama's supposed basis in dialogue in works like *Play* and *Krapp's Last Tape*, but the technique reaches a more extreme form in *Not I*, where the isolated Mouth doggedly persists in using the third person to recount the experiences of a 'tiny little girl' in a nameless 'godforsaken hole'.[12] Here, Beckett offers us his most emphatic negation of a fundamental aspect of conventional dramatic dialogue, its basis in an *I-you* relationship between speaker and listener.[13]

Semioticians like Alessandro Serpieri have pointed out that, among the literary genres, the drama exhibits the most rigid and stable reliance on generic conventions[14], and one might logically include among these conventions those associated with dramatic dialogue. As its very title makes clear, *Not I* deliberately omits the generic technique of first person speech, transforming this convention into what might therefore be called a 'minus function'.[15] Because this convention is so much a part of audience expectations, its omission has the ultimate effect of calling up 'in the mind of the [spectator] exactly those procedures which the text avoids using'.[16] On one level, the denial of the first person thus incites the spectator to restore it; we project that very *I* which the speaker so carefully avoids using, assuming that the narrated story is in fact Mouth's own despite her (or its) repeated denials.

Yet this experiment with dialogue does more than merely elicit our participation in Mouth's act of storytelling. It also guides our response to the play by inviting us to consider the reasons behind Mouth's 'vehement refusal to relinquish third person'.[17] Here we see the workings of two different strategies for shaping audience response. The 'minus function' or denial of dialogue conventions may push us to reflect on the relationship of those conventions to the dramatic medium itself, to recognise, for example, what William B. Worthen describes as 'the vital duplicity of acting'.[18] Even for the most perfectly trained method actor, there always remains a gap between the self and the role being played; Mouth's refusal to become the *I* of the rambling story deftly sums up this situation of role playing.

What Wolfgang Iser calls 'negativity' also comes into play here, a device which signals 'those deformations of the human condition and those failures of human action present in literary texts whilst, at the same time, drawing the reader's attention to the unformulated causes of such deformations and failures'.[19] Our formulations of the causes of Mouth's strange behaviour in *Not I* will doubtless take different shapes according to each spectator's individual disposition. We may see the escape into the third person as Mouth's means of 'running away from . . . its own bête noir',[20] for example, or as a 'fierce and deeply human judgement on the desolation and solitude of the barren life that [Mouth] is forced to recount'.[21] In each case, though, the simple device of emphasising the usually unmarked third person both engages and orients audience participation in the theatrical experience prefigured in Beckett's dramatic text. And if, as Keir Elam suggests, 'much of the audience's pleasure derives from the continual effort to discover the principles at work' in an innovative theatrical text,[22] our recognition of this dialogic innovation may even account for some of our delight in viewing Beckett's demanding playlet.

But whatever meaning we might ascribe to Mouth's refusal of the first person depends not only on Beckett's unconventional dialogue but also on that disembodied figure's position on the stage. As Anne Ubersfeld argues, 'the "meaning" of an utterance in the theatre, putting the situation of communication aside, is absolutely nothing; only that situation allowing the conditions of speech to be established gives the utterance its sense' (my translation).[23] Fundamental to our reception of the dramatic and theatrical work, then, is not only the *I-you* relationship between the speakers but also the *here-and-now*, the concrete space within which the actor-characters appear before the audience. And the scenic experiments of Beckett's later plays point to the audience's central role in establishing the speech situation of his characters as they appear within the concrete space of his stage settings.

Consider, for example, the powerful visual images of *A Piece of Monologue*, where a white-haired, white-robed Speaker shares the stage with a pallet bed and a lamp with a 'skull-sized white globe'.[24] In performance, the bed, lamp, and other paraphernalia of the setting and lighting to some extent constitute the character's speech situation for us. Yet *A Piece of Monologue* makes clear the refusal of both the written and the staged texts to spell out the precise links between a play's verbal and non-verbal elements. In so doing, it highlights the extent to which these links must be forged by the spectator.

Once again using the third peron, Beckett's Speaker begins 'Birth was the death of him' and goes on to tell a highly fragmented story of a life extending 'From funeral to funeral'.[25] Scattered throughout the account are references to 'Gown and socks white to take faint light . . . Foot of pallet just visible edge of frame . . . Pale globe alone in gloom' until, as the dim scenic lamplight becomes still dimmer, the Speaker comments, 'the light going now. Beginning to go. In the room. Where else?'[26] This fragmented speech may in itself compel the spectator to connect various segments of the story; but its scattered references 'To now. This night'[27] and to the main features of the play's stark set underline the extent which even this fragmented 'discourse is geared to the stage situation'[28] from which the Speaker at first appears to be divorced. Like *Not I*, *A Piece of Monologue* manoeuvres the audience to bridge the gap between the teller and his tale, but this time we do so by linking the Speaker and his words to his actual speech situation. As the play unfolds on the stage, *we* associate the Speaker's words with the sparse yet detailed setting, relating his white socks and nightgown to those of the character in the story and the 'now' of the narrative to the moment of the actual performance. Once again, Beckett's drama brings to light a fundamental aspect of theatrical communication, showing how the play's 'global spatio-temporal structure is constructed by the spectator *for himself* from the uneven bits of perceptual data that he receives'.[29]

As with many of Beckett's later plays, the disparate fragments of *A Piece of Monologue* come together to form a concrete stage image, in this case an image of humanity 'Dying on', as the Speaker says.[30] Critics have often commented on the importance of such visual images to Beckett's drama but the tension between the supposedly off-stage world evoked in the Speaker's narrative and the on-stage world visible to the audience in this particular play helps clarify their impact on Beckett's spectator. For while the power of such images does indeed stem from their ability to theatrically distill a particular life situation, it also arises from the audience's involvement in resolving the tension between word and image, between the staged events and the recounted ones, by making their own connections between the play's verbal and scenic dimension. The poignancy of *A Piece of Monologue*'s image of 'Dying on', in other words, becomes more intense as we ourselves situate the narrated events and objects within the room we see on stage, identifying the third-person story as the Speaker's own, recognising the solitary, fading light as a scenic double for the Speaker's solitary death, and then, perhaps, relating that image to the end point of our own lives.

Moreover, if we rush too quickly to formulate an interpretation of this brief play as a visual metaphor for the solitary process of dying (or whatever other meaning we might construct), we risk overlooking the power of the scenic image itself. If, as Martin Esslin argues, what the audience should take home from viewing a play like *A Piece of*

Monologue is 'the *overall impact* of a single overwhelmingly powerful image',[31] it is important to recognise the density of these images—the fact that they are built up from an intricate and highly varied 'communicational system'[32]—and the implications of this density for audience response.

Speaking of *Footfalls*, Beckett insisted on the centrality of another of his stage images, that of the dishevelled May, endlessly pacing across the front of the stage. According to Beckett, 'this was [my] basic conception . . . the text, the words were only built up around this picture. . . . That is the centre of the play, everything else is secondary'.[33] Beckett's remark suggests that his texts themselves regulate our responses to these dense theatrical images and *Footfalls* reveals several additional facets of this process. To begin with, as he did in *Not I* and *That Time*, Beckett here presents his audience with but a fragment of a human body. While the rest of May may be dimly visible, *Footfalls* emphasises May's feet pacing up and down. Like the fragmentation of his characters' stories and the verbal references to off-stage characters and events, this fragmentation of their bodies hints at the existence of a larger picture. It induces us to fill it in, to visualise in our own imaginations the whole signified by these body parts.

At the same time, the play marshals an entire repertoire of staging devices—including lighting, costume, sound, and movement—to fix our gaze not only on a specific figure (or part of one) but also, on that particular part of the stage on which May stands, paces, and 'wheels'. In so doing, Beckett's staging underlines the role played by our perception of theatrical space, giving support to Elam's assertion that 'the theatrical text is defined and perceived above all in spatial terms'.[34] Yet, whereas more conventional theatre may leave the spectator's eye relatively free to roam about the stage, to take in details of setting, costume, and gesture from various areas of the theatrical space, a play like *Footfalls* limits and directs our perception in a manner that more closely approximates the eye of the camera in film. Or, to draw another analogy, Beckett's staging works to constrain the gaze of his audience much as it often painfully restricts the movement of his actors.

Nevertheless, while our field of vision may be narrowed, the overall theatrical experience *Footfalls* offers us once again remains extremely dense. The *sight* of May's pacing, turning, stopping and pacing again; the *sounds* of her footfalls, the echoing chime, and the two women's voices; and the *actions* performed by each character's words, constitute a variety of what Iser calls 'textual perspectives', which vie for our awareness during the time-flow of the performance. According to Iser's theory of reader response, the reader's switching back and forth among perspectives and the process of combing these perspectives into a 'referential field', ultimately leads to the formation of the 'aesthetic object' of the text. If Iser's own examples of this process are any indication, this 'object' amounts to a basically intellectual realisation about human nature or about those social or literary norms which have been selected for the reader's attention.[35]

But as *Footfalls* progresses, the powerful image of May's measured pacing almost seems to preclude, or perhaps even transcend purely intellectual reflection. Comments like the Voice's 'Will you never have done . . . revolving it all? . . . In your poor mind'[36], the repeated counting of May's steps, and the verbal references to the floor on which she walks, all work to bring this image itself to the foreground, suggesting that the theatrical experience of Beckett's spectator may be much more than the purely intellectual one that a theory like Iser's describes. According to James Knowlson, Beckett's London production of *Footfalls* 'seems, in fact, to have been shaped to evoke feelings of distress, strangeness and mystery, a sense of inexplicable seeking, and yet the distillation of absence and loss'.[37] Upon leaving a performance of *Footfalls*, we may well find ourselves, like May, 'revolving' in our 'poor minds' the words, images, and actions we have heard and seen. But by concentrating our attention on concrete images like that of May's dragging feet, Beckett's plays often haunt us with an evocative picture rather than an absorbing idea.

Moreover, the 'intricate interplay between movement and speech'[38] characterizing a play like *Footfalls* reminds us that whereas the reading of a novel is a relatively sequential process, the theatrical performance introduces a variety of signs simultaneously competing for the spectator's attention. Many of these signs, as we have already noted in discussing both *Footfalls* and *A Piece of Monologue*, are visual or perceptual in nature; and even the plays' fragmented narratives are often distilled to their most evocative details, as if Beckett had deleted 'all but the most essentially visual portion of what might be a long descriptive paragraph' (Esslin)[39]. 'The globe alone', says the Speaker of *Monologue*[40], while May in *Footfalls* describes the heroine of her story passing 'before the candelabrum, how its flames, their light . . . like moon through passing rack'.[41] This perceptual density, coupled with Beckett's peculiar overlapping of word pictures and scenic images, not only allows one code or system of signs to be played off against another in the spectator's imagination, it also provides a clue to the experience of 'strangeness and mystery' Knowlson discusses and contributes to the multi-dimensional or polyphonic quality of Beckett's later plays.

Returning to the example of *A Piece of Monologue*, we find what Ruby Cohn describes as 'a still life unveiled by the parting of a curtain'.[42] As the play progresses, we discover that the apparent coalescence of word and image discussed above is broken by contradictions—between the oil lamp in the story and the electric one on stage, for example, or between the extremely active figure of the narrative and the essentially immobile Speaker.[43] Yet Beckett compels us to hold several different aspects of the play in our minds at once, to scan the stage at the same time that we are listening to the story. We are asked to view this theatrical 'still life' much the way the artist views his canvas, using what Paul Klee has called scattered or 'multi-dimensional' attention.[44]

This type of looking 'overcomes the conscious division of the object of our perception into figure and ground'[45] by attending to both aspects of the object—to both the figure and its background or, in this case, to both the words and the scenic images—at once. Unlike normal or 'focussed attention', which organises the field of perception into a logical hierarchy, Klee's scattered or 'unfocused attention' thus involves a very different mental framework, a kind of 'absence of mind' operating outside our everyday, intellectual processes. Instead of conscious logic, then, plays like *A Piece of Monologue* engage a paradoxically 'full' emptiness of attention.[46]

In arguing that knowledge only begins with sensations, which then converge to form images and finally abstract ideas, our Western philosophical tradition has tended to value the concept much more highly than the percept or sensation.[47] Beckett's theatre appears to work against this valuation. By carefully layering stark visual images, sounds, and often only vaguely understandable dialogue, by confronting us with a clash of word and image or with substantial gaps between what is seen and what is said, Beckett's theatre inundates us with percepts. It thereby presents his particular vision of the world in a what Klee would call a polyphonic manner, one which forestalls our formation of abstract concepts by challenging us to perceive the different strands of his theatrical works simultaneously, much as the trained listener scatters his attention over all of the strains of a complex musical structure. Just as Beckett has tended to efface the presence of biographical detail in revising his writing (cf. Gontarski),[48] so he has worked to eclipse the intellectual aspect of audience responses to his plays. The later plays, especially, underscore Ubersfeld's assertion that 'the theatre exists to *speak*, but also to *be* . . . the theatre is seen before it is understood'.[49]

It is tempting to read the recent *What Where* as mirroring this undermining of the intellectual in Beckett's theatre. Consider those four figures, Bam, Bem, Bim, and Bom, who 'give . . . the works' to those who refuse to say 'it', to say 'where', and to say where he said 'where'. Could they not be likened to those critics who 'torture' Beckett's texts to 'mean something', as Hamm says to Clov in *Endgame*? Who demand of each other an explanation of 'where' Beckett said 'it . . . And what' he said? All Beckett's Voice (in both senses of the possessive) can really say, it appears, is that 'Time passes' (yet another reminder that 'Something is taking its course', to return to *Endgame* once again?). And so the Voice of *What Where* challenges us to 'Make sense who may' as it 'switch[es] off'.[50] Yet, just as the different musical strains of a symphony interweave to form a sound much richer than the dominant melody, so the words emanating from *What Where*'s grey megaphone blend with the scenic permutations of Bam and his fellows to form a theatrical work offering much more than this simple concept of passing time.

In their polyphonic insistence on the drama's material aspects, Beckett's later plays speak that language 'addressed first of all to the senses instead of being addressed primarily to the mind' demanded in Artaud's *The Theatre and Its Double*.[51] By minimising dialogue, plot, and characterization while maximizing what Aristotle called 'spectacle', these plays challenge us to recognise their violations of dramatic conventions. They also force us to build our own bridges between word and image. And they make us grapple with the frustration of 'looking for sense', as one of the women in *Play* puts it, 'where possibly there is none'.[52] But are these qualities in fact unique or do Beckett's plays merely intensify the essential aspects of any theatrical experience?

Beckett's particular formula for intellectual teasing and sensory stimulation may well illustrate the 'general trend . . . *through* and *beyond* intellectualism, towards experience' which Una Chaudhuri sees as characteristic of modern Western drama.[53] But the intense physicality of Beckett's experiments in scenic narration highlights the fundamental mode of *all* theatre, the telling of its stories through the mediation of concrete objects and live performers. In so doing, these experiments reveal the limitations of a theory of audience response focussed primarily on the intellectual or philosophical dimensions of the theatrical experience. And in making us aware of the theatre's 'polyphony', and the peculiar type of attention such density induces,

Beckett's later plays do not set themselves apart from the mainstream of Western dramatic literature. Rather, to paraphrase Victor Shklovsky's assessment of *Tristram Shandy*,[54] Beckett's are the most typical plays in all of world theatre.

MUTATIONS OF THE SOLILOQUY—*NOT I* TO *ROCKABY*

ANDREW KENNEDY

The late plays of Beckett, from *Not I* on, create a significantly new type of theatre, new both in relation to all previous drama and in relation to Beckett's earlier plays. Anyone can see that we have been given further and radical instances of dramatic 'lessness': miniature monodramas that pursue a principle of self-diminishment, that is, the self moving towards existential and verbal extinction. That direction is inherent in the perfected movement of Beckett's total work, in what might be called a controlled inward regression. Nevertheless, the plays I am concerned with move nearer the *end*—Beckett's asymptotic curve has reached the line that marks the limits of art in dramatic language. In their reaching towards last things and last sayings (or un-saying), the late plays also reach—through the customary lessening of dramatic action, character and language—far beyond the known limits of the traditional soliloquy.[1]

I start with this emphasis for, just as some of the most innovatory features of Beckett's plays become more visible when seen to be *leaning against* known dramatic conventions, so the achievement of certain late plays becomes more visible when seen to be leaning against the particular convention of the soliloquy. As behind the cyclic structures of the early plays lies our communal sense of linear action; behind the immobilised stage figure (rooted in dustbin, sand-mound or urn) and the round naturalistic character, and behind the well-shaped stichomythia or incantatory rhythm, the supposed norms of mimetic speech—so behind the speaking voice[s] in Beckett's new kind of monodrama we hear the I-centred soliloquy we know from Shakespeare to Beckett: Beckett before these late mutations. The retreat from the grammar of the speaking 'I' is accompanied by a retreat from most of the familiar structures and topics of the old self-dramatising rhetoric. The developing new mode presents the non-self in a no-longer soliloquy.

In Western drama the soliloquy has gradually come to be identified with 'inner speech' or 'self-discourse',[2] expressing a certain sensibility, pivoting on the consciously voiced experiences of the speaking 'I'. This can be said despite the many choric and reflective soliloquies, in Shakespeare and the Jacobean dramatists, with collective plural pronouns ('Thus conscience does make cowards of us all'). The directly self-expressive 'I' may be replaced by self-apostrophe but *not*—as far as I know—by the third person. When Viola in *Twelfth Night* II.iv, speaks of herself as *she* ('She never told her love . . .') it is a framed speech-of-disguise, spoken to the Duke, with the audience implicated in the speech strategy. Even the character who questions his identity, Hamlet *par excellence*, will hitch his shaken self-command to the grammar and rhetoric of the central 'I' pronoun ('O what a rogue and peasant slave am I!' *Hamlet*, II.ii), while the mad character, or the character on the brink of madness like Lear, will utter extreme feelings in broken syntax but cling to the pivotal pronoun ('I will do such things-/What they are, yet I know not'—*King Lear*, II.,iv). If anything, the fragmented self, the no longer solid ego, is shored up by the grammatical stability of the 'I'-voice, with its rhetorical overkill, moving towards mono-maniac monologue.

Now these observations apply also to Beckett's drama before *Not I*. In a bird's eye-view; after the ingeniously varied duologues of *Waiting for Godot* and *Endgame*, came the shadow-dialogue of selves in *Krapp's Last Tape* and the self-transcending dialogue of Winnie in *Happy Days*, each anchored to surging self-reflection carried by the omnipresent 'I'voice. Even in *Play*, those ghosted voices, claiming to be no longer in our space-time, cling to the comforts of the first person singular. The exception is the grammar of Lucky who uses no 'I'-pronoun (except in the mechanically repeated 'I resume'—phrase, clearly a functional connective devoid of self-expression: 'I resume alas alas'). Lucky is probably one of the precursors of the non-I voices in the late monodramas.[3]

The 'I'-voice is the pivot of self-expressive speech in life, in drama, just as the 'I-you' exchange is the axis of all verbal interactions both in daily conversation and in dramatic dialogue. Long before contemporary theatre semiotics (Serpieri and Elam)[4] has re-emphasised the importance of deixis including the personal pronoun, in the languages of drama, Roman Jakobson warned that a minimal use of the personal pronoun may be a sign of madness—witness Hölderlin's late poetry.[5] The linguist and the semiotician is supported by certain psychiatric studies of schizophrenia, notably case histories interpreted by R. D. Laing in *The Divided Self* (1959). The patient called Peter dreaded any question whatever that might require an 'I'-statement from him. Avoidance of such a statement became a way of life, what Laing calls 'an intentional project of self-annihilation'. Such patients 'had come to feel more and more convinced that it was a mere pretence . . . to be somebody and that the only honest course they could take was to become nobody, since that was all they could feel themselves "really" to be'.[6]

The new grammar, transforming the 'I' pronoun into SHE (*Not I*), YOU (*That Time*), and into a residual SHE among pronounless 'rocking' phrases (*Rockaby*), turns would-be soliloquisers into strange new narrators. Dramatic speech then takes on certain features of an *as if* narrative; on the one hand abandoning the self-aware and self-expressive character, on the other hand not presenting an autonomous fictional 'hero' with a story and consciousness distinct from the narrator's condition. Rather, the narrator is like the solipsistic self impersonating a broken autobiography. The formal vocal monologue (one actor speaking) remains, but the new non-I voice clings to mere remnants of the old soliloquy: to certain topics and tones, for instance the urgent confessional utterance of *Not I*, the compulsion to recall an indefinite and overlapping past in *That Time*, and a wholly new kind of dying speech in *Rockaby*. The attempt to 'tell a story', to impersonate 'somebody', nevertheless is shot through with a 'monologic outlook', to borrow Bakhtin's term for a narrative that does not create a plural word—where 'the *other*/person/ remains entirely and only an *object* of consciousness, and cannot constitute another consciousness'.[7] In other words, the *as if* narrator abandons, along with the 'I'-voice, the desire or capacity to imagine a person 'out there' and distinct from itself, just as it abandons the capacity for direct self-revelation to an audience, other than a shadowy Auditor, a visible but silent *alter ego*.

Not I is the first no-longer soliloquy, paradoxically drawing on the resources of the traditional soliloquy which it renounces and transforms. In particular, we are challenged by the anguished suppression of the grammatical 'I' at the centre of a dramatic speech in which the hidden 'I' of the suffering old woman still struggles towards self-recognition. The critic, long familiar with the text, may take this tension—between the suppressed and the emerging speaker—as given. But the audience, in the actual conditions of a first performance, will experience the *process* of terrible non-self-revelation as a cryptic ordeal. Perhaps all the five variant repetitions of the Mouth's 'vehement refusal to relinquish the third person'[8] are needed for an audience to see the pattern in the drama of the dislocated 'I'-pronoun:

> not knowing what . . . what she was—. . . what? . . . who? . . . no! . . . she! . . . SHE![9]

It is the last of five fragmented utterances and comes with the clarity of a cry, and the ambiguity of an oracle (the last one coming nearest to pointing to total agnosticism concerning selfhood: 'not knowing what . . . what she was'). By then the play is almost ended, and it has probably taken the whole play to identify the SHE with the NOT-I of the title. (At least one reviewer confessed to missing that insight altogether.)[10] Only '*gradually*/altogether/do we/ realise that we are hearing not fiction but autobiography, that Mouth is . . . relating the details of her own life, describing to us her present situation, a fact she tries desperately to disguise by narrating in the third person'—in Hersh Zeifman's words, my emphasis.[11]

To put it another way, whilst in Hamlet's 'To be or not to be' speech the general reflections on existence and the death-wish are at once seen to reflect Hamlet (even though the I-pronoun is not once uttered in the soliloquy), in the Mouth's rapid and multi-layered speech-flow the links between the speaker and her speech are deliberately discontinuous, flickering signals from a faulty lighthouse. Shakespeare uses the formal convention of the soliloquy as a sign-posted platform for something new to be said by the protagonist. Beckett uses the Mouth's struggle *against* self-speech (that is, soliloquy) for something new, to be barely said, through that new speech-form that has no previous existence or name.

Yet it is not so much the formal invention as the apparently self-expressive intensity in the language—and its delivery—that alerts us to certain features of soliloquising in Mouth's speech-flow. There is the sheer subjectivity of her *as if* narrative, transcending any external story-telling and even empathy—the Ancient Mariner compulsion, let us say. Intimate details of private experience are being disclosed: lovelessness, non-enjoyment of sex, the agony of being deprived of speech and the agony of speech suddenly recovered. The story of crisis opens out towards sudden vision ('God is love') which is affirmed and mocked, with an inward kind of testimony. Theme, tone and rhythm together point to one suffering person; her confessional urgency is played in the key of soliloquy, Mouth exhibits the feverish disturbance she speaks of; from beginning to end her speech is iconic. And the audience is caught up in that pathos, on the level of speech dynamics, before conscious understanding and judgement. Insight into one aspect of her situation comes later: by killing the 'I'-voice, the true soliloquy, Mouth is attempting self-slaughter. Self-discovery compels self-blinding in the Oedipus paradigm; for Mouth it compels the dislocation of the essential 'I'—soliloquy deformed/transformed.

That Time lay 'on the very edge of what was possible in the theatre', in Beckett's own words,[12] and it also places the soliloquy on the very edge of its dramatic possibilities. (Here I shall restrict myself to a few tentative observations, as I have, unfortunately, been unable to see, or hear a sound recording of, this play). The conversion of the 'I' into 'You' is less of a dislocation than the 'I' into 'She' in *Not I*; self-apostrophe is in keeping with a certain linguistic and poetic convention. Nor is this pronoun-shift and self-suppression struggled for in the manner of MOUTH, and it does not constitute a dramatic core in itself (even though the You-address is effective). At the same time the partial blurring of the three shades of speech (A, B and C in permutation) deliberately *lessens* the distinctness of three phases in the life of the Listener, the 'owner' of the three voices (in contrast to the dynamic dialogue of selves in *Krapps Last Tape*).[13] The soliloquising urge is recaptured but the soliloquy suffers another sea-change. The change is in two directions. Existentially, the experiences all create a stasis; memories freed from all desire, with the mode of elegy dominant, and inner drama spent. (This could be tested in certain episodes, for instance in the love-vow—B2—and in seeing his image in the picture's glass—C3—, though the latter comes nearest to a crisis of self-recognition.) Vocally, the intercalated, prerecorded voices take to a further point that automatic speech which has earlier, partial versions in Lucky, in the tape of young Krapp, and in the voices in *Play*. So the cumulative concentration on shadowy reminiscences in a final, internally layered, soliloquy is reinforced by puppet-speech (a possible version of Kleist's marionette theatre[14]), and significantly opposed to the 'thinking aloud' aspect of the traditional soliloquy.

It is in *Rockaby* (1981), it seems to me, that the problem of a final soliloquy is solved as a supreme miniature drama. The constituent elements are all attuned; the compressed tender plot, tracing the steps of retreat towards death; the distilled 'purity of diction' based on Anglo-Saxon monosyllables, and creating an affinity between the language of the child and that of senescence and dying; and, unifying all, the rocking rhythm which transmutes the panting rhythm we know from *Cascando* and *Not I* into something new. All this is anchored to the stage image of the 'prematurely old' woman ('Unkempt grey hair. Huge eyes in white expressionless face. White hands holding ends of armrests.'—stage direction) rocking herself towards and into death—a rite comparable to Peer Gynt driving his mother towards death in a sledge.

The compressed plot includes a thread that evokes the woman's longing for 'another' and her failure to encounter such a one, until her retreat into final solitude is compelled:

time she went right down
was her own other
other living soul
so in the end
close of a long day
went down
let down the blind and down
right down
into the old rocker[15]

These lines enact an inner drama in which total isolation is made to seem inevitable, in terms of the feeling and the final stage in a five-step withdrawal from the outward-directed self. Here the solipsistic soliloquy is, as it were, given its genesis. (One can see it as the counterpart of the origin of dialogue in the self splitting into voices, 'the solitary child who turns himself into children, two, three . . .' *Endgame*, p. 45.) In the end, one voice only is possible. Here the voice in the woman's head and the 'voice over' are fused in a soliloquy so inward, self-renouncing and hyponotic that—after the one curse: 'fuck life'—its slow fade-out, too, seems inevitable. And perhaps that marks the final mutation of the soliloquy—in Beckett, in drama.

ANONYMITY AND INDIVIDUATION: THE INTERRELATION OF TWO LINGUISTIC FUNCTIONS IN *NOT I* AND *ROCKABY*

LOIS OPPENHEIM

I

'The danger', claimed Beckett, 'is in the neatness of the identification. The conception of Philosophy and Philology as a pair of nigger minstrels out of Teatro dei Piccoli is soothing, like the contemplation of a carefully folded ham-sandwich.'[1] In recent years, in the wake of the infusion of structural linguistics in the domain of narrative function, the post-structuralist undoing of textuality as a unified, signifying presence has done its best to subvert this identification and, in so doing, it has not only focused attention on the fundamentally specious nature of the 'scientific' interpretation of literary language, but rendered more manifest the danger of any critical method choosing to ignore the ontological transparency of language in favour of its apparently non-perceptual or material opacity.

A review of Beckett criticism published in recent years reveals the contrasts which, evolving from the disassociation of the minstrel pair, have come to define the struggle between a theoretical orientation which holds that the systematic differentiation of linguistic forms or the establishment of a hierarchy of structural oppositions is undermined as a critical tool by semantic function itself and a hermeneutic which evaluates narrative or poetic discourse *not* in accordance with either the communicative autonomy of expression (viewed as a system of fully invested signs) or its ultimate undoing by an intervention operating *within that very system itself*, but with the *deformation* of assumed (arbitrarily determined) structural and semantic hierarchies.

In an astute evaluation of Beckett's *Not I*, for example, Keir Elam writes of the playwright's progressive movement away from 'a full semantic or expressive investment in the sign',[2] indicating a possible privileging of the non-mediated or direct—which is to say perceptual and intersubjective—experiencing of Beckett's language. Elam's definition of rhetoric 'as the art of the what-not' ('. . . what matters is not so much what is put in as what is strategically left out')[3], however, allows the critic to return to a tropological analysis, one which incorporates—in a metaphysics of absence—both synedoche, as a 'figure of reduction, of the lesser *in praesentia* that stands for the greater *in assentia*',[4] and litotes, 'a figure of negative affirmation'.[5] Elam's effort to display these 'alternative' or 'negative' rhetorical categories for Beckett's 'dramatic figurations' do 'still presuppose . . . the semantic integrity of the sign', Elam tells us, insofar as 'both synedoche and litotes function only if what is shown is taken to stand for something *other* than itself'.[6]

Philosopher Eugene Kaelin, on the other hand, comes somewhat closer to divesting the sign of its semantic fullness in coming to terms both with the opaque structural relationships of signifier and signified—the totality of the linguistic context whose closure may either be 'felt' by the reader or 'raised to the level of understanding'[7]—and the transparent ontological functioning of language in Beckett. He does so by proclaiming the critical task to be one of describing the *implicit* structures of the fiction. In a distinctly non-deconstructive vein, Kaelin refers to his method of opening the closed or saturated sign system as a 'phenomenological structuralism' in which all reference to a priori conceptualization and presupposed theoretical points of departure are said to be 'bracketed' (à la Husserl) from his 'hermeneutical expansion' of the general linguistic context. For Kaelin, it is the ontic experiences of Beckett's personages, 'the experience of being in their worlds', which reveal the ontological structures or 'basic principles by which everyday human experiences are understood to be possible in the first place'.[8] Thus Kaelin goes farther than Elam in subverting the objectivation of meaning by choosing not to deconstruct the signifier through the metaphysical presencing of negativity or absence, but to seek the 'literary depth structures'[9] or the primary *potentiality* of words to mean. Indeed, Kaelin goes farther than many Beckett critics in investigating the fundamental endowment of language and linguistic imagery with the primordial relation of the writer to the world. This is to say that Kaelin succeeds where Elam does not insofar as his focus is maintained on the author and his narrative or dramatic personages as speaking subjects who are the subjects of a linguistic praxis. It is in the work of yet another Beckett devotee, however, that the question of a truly unmediated mode of linguistic experience is most fully explored, a question which neither the thematisation of the schism between cognitive and corporeal function in the overwhelming majority of Beckett's texts nor its elucidation in the corpus of Beckett criticism, can continue to conceal.

Lance St. John Butler's study, *Samuel Beckett and the Meaning of Being*,[10] is undoubtedly the most comprehensive consideration of Beckett's work in the context of pure ontology. This highly intelligent evaluation of the author in the light of Heidegger, Sartre and Hegel offers a way into Beckett that depends not so much on a philosophically informed analysis of Beckett's language as a semiotic system, as in Kaelin's work *An Unhappy Consciousness*, but on the notion of language as the metaphoric correlate and that of fiction as the allegorical equivalent of the *In-der-Welt-sein* (or Being-in-the-World).

The significance of this work for an in-depth investigation of Beckett's plays *Not I* and *Rockaby* resides in Butler's effort to situate his analysis of the Self, as the subject of Beckett's work, on the level of an analysis of the 'revealability' of language: the ability of the word to reveal Being both in the positive dimension of its potentiality and the negative counterpart of its sum possibilities, facticity. For, insofar as it is on the level of the opening of semantic function onto the ontico-ontological dimension of Being that the profoundly perceptual nature of the literary or creative imagination is uncovered, Beckett's preoccupation with speech and the Voice as synonomous with existence may be said to reveal a dialectical process as yet unexplored by Beckett criticism.

The failure of the Self to reach an integrated status has long been regarded by readers of Beckett as the most consistently valid context in which to view the psycho-social insufficiencies exemplified by this author's characterizations. Butler's analysis of Beckett's texts as 'ontological parables' and of Beckett's discourse as the creation of 'metaphysical possibilities', however, appears to support our contention that the dissolution of the ego is an unnecessarily reductive formulation by which to evaluate both the syntactic and thematic impotence that particularize and unify the form and content of Beckett's work. It is thus in the light of this critic's study, and specifically the chapter entitled 'Heidegger's *Being and Time* and Beckett',[11] that we propose an alternative context for interpretation: the dialectical interplay between anonymity—or the linguistic unveiling of the universal structures of Being—and individuation—the verbal process by which the ego both differentiates itself from all that it is not and becomes progressively self-aware. And it will be our purpose in the following pages to explore some facets of the inter--

relation of these two linguistic functions as they operate in Beckett's two recent plays.

II

A preliminary investigation of both *Not I* and *Rockaby* reveals that the seemingly irrational or nonsensical language of these two plays is a function of a representational reading, one which views literary language as the sign or symbol of some existential order existing beyond or outside of the text. Labelled 'Absurd' as a consequence of such a reading, Beckett's language has all too often been stripped of its most unique aesthetic qualities, to say nothing of its inherent ontology, as the decoding of images has led to what Elam refers to as 'some spot-on existential-condition exercise'.[12] In re-situating the language of these plays on an order of reference other than that of representation, and specifically on the order of the intentionality of consciousness (whereby subject and object are fused in a perceptual mode), a more valid understanding may be achieved in which semantic and syntactic disintegration are no longer viewed as either paradigmatic or emblematic of a progressively disintegrated psyche.

Our first indications that Beckett's language—regarded in accordance with an intentional rather than a representational order of linguistic function—would yield a more profound understanding than that accorded by the rationalist critic to a supposedly 'irrationalist' discourse are the very first utterances in each of the plays. In *Not I*, it is the unintelligible sounds made by Mouth from behind the curtain, as well as the omission, from the initial intelligible sounds, of key words necessary for a grammatically complete construction, that provokes the reader or spectator to relinquish that safe distance from the fictive universe traditionally maintained by the representational view of art. In *Rockaby*, it is the use of a connecting word, 'till' ('till in the end/the day came'), a preposition having, as the first word of the play, no preceding element to which to relate what follows, that produces a similar reaction. It is the absence of any real beginning in each of the plays, in other words, which allows for the immediate apprehension of the enigmatic structure—erroneously identified as Absurd—of Beckett's world. Entering the texts through the absence of *decipherable* speech in *Not I* and the absence of *predicative or declarative* speech at the start of *Rockaby* projects the reader or viewer—like the 'tiny little thing', the 'tiny little girl' that was Mouth—'. . . out . . . into this world . . .,'[13] *in media res*, tearing him from his habitual, rational orientation towards language, in which textual meaning is thought to represent the world, and implanting him, *ipso facto*, on the level of the intentional functioning of language where the integration of consciousness with the world precludes its representation and reveals perception as the foundation of imaginative discourse.

It is this interruption, this rupturing of language as the logical and referential positing of a reality outside the text, one whose designation is prerequisite in ordinary discourse to the semantic unfolding of words, which yields from the start, the awareness of a syntactic uncertainty, of a paradigmatic deformation, from within which the very images that constitute the drama emerge. Dislocation, discontinuity and disproportion then, are the only syntactic and syntagmatic rules of the game, and they are precisely those which both preclude the reduction of a network of images to an objectified unity, a material text, and suspend the reader on a level of understanding where preconception and presupposition of the world, and the self's relation to it, are irrelevant.

Consider, for example, that from the first words of *Not I* emerges the image of this 'tiny little girl', projected 'before her time' into this 'godforsaken hole' that is, at once, the fathomless space of our world *and* that orifice whose very presence is the *dramatis persona* herself of the text. The image of Mouth is constituted both thematically and structurally, as opposed to symbolically or metonymically, therefore, by the unification of a verbal irruption of 'something': namely, sound and meaning, *and* its opposite, 'nothing': ellipsis, lacuna—preventing the reader from attributing the closed or totalizing system of symbolic reproduction to what is more accurately deemed a dynamic and creative opening, that of the transcendental imagination unfolding onto the horizon of the perceptual world.

Similarly, in *Rockaby*, the careful synchronisation of the aurally perceptible voice with the visually perceptible rocking of the woman in her chair precludes interpretation on the order of symbolic representation. While one might be tempted, initially, to view the dichotomy of the female character in terms of a disintegration of the Self—the woman in her rocker experiencing, ontologically, her own potentiality, the tape of her voice constituting, ontically, the facticity of her Being—a more careful reading reveals that it is *not* the *Self* that is bifurcated in Beckett's dramatisation, the ontico-ontological dimension of Dasein being the two sides of a same coin, but rather *the Self's perception of reality*: the exaggerated—for the purpose of heightening the drama—*incongruence* of a cognitive and pre-cognitive awareness of the world.

In *Not I*, moreover, it is Mouth's refusal to unite herself with the first-person pronominal expression of individuality as, in *Rockaby*, it is the woman's search 'for another/another living soul/one other living soul/going to and fro/all eyes like herself . . .',[14] that maintains the force of the fiction as an ontological, and thereby non-representational, parable. Considered according to the *oppositions* to which representational thinking on art gives rise—real and imaginary, mind and matter, man and the objective world, words and the concrete realities they are thought to reiterate, or translate from a silent to an expressive mode of being—[15] Mouth's 'vehement refusal to relinquish the third person'[16] has been variously and rationally interpreted as 'a fierce and deeply human judgement on the desolation and solitude of the barren life that she is forced to recount . . .'[17] as the determination 'to obliterate any relationship with [her] own agonizing past',[18] as the 'disassociation of the self from the category of individuality'.[19] Considered according to the *unifications* that art, re-situated on the order on intentionality, unveils, however, the real problem posed by Beckett may be said to reside *neither* in the devaluation of life (and hence its qualification as 'Absurd') *nor* in the insufficient resources of the self for integration, but in the fundamental impossibility of any true identification of the self *for the self* either apart from a relation to the Other or in connection with the Other. It is to that extent that Being is always a Being-there, a Being-in-the-World, posed, in the mode of its ecstatic consciousness, at a distance from itself, fully conscious of itself *only* in its relation to the world into which it is intentionally thrown, that the first person pronoun appears both denotatively and connotatively inadequate and Mouth's rejection of it becomes meaningful. In Butler's words:

> 'I' is inadequate, in both Heidegger and Beckett, as a term for the Self, merely indicating in both cases that we are dealing with Dasein for whom the world is always 'mine'.[20]

Taking this analysis a step farther, Mouth's insistence on 'she' as opposed to 'I' appears less significantly a thematisation of the inability of the self to integrate than a *metaphoric correlation* of language with the intentionalising structure of consciousness, that which negates the empiricism of a pure subjectivity ('I') in favour of the transcendental call to the universality of Being ('I' as 'she'). In this perspective, Mouth transforms the empirical self of Beckett's early fiction into the transcendental self of the Unnamable, the self of Molloy, via that of Malone, into her own immediate predecessor, one who, as 'I'—in the deficient pronominal expression of the transcendental nature of Dasein—given way to 'she' substantiating the 'JE est un autre' of Rimbaud, and unveiling that tension between individuality and anonymity that underlies Beckett's entire fictional enterprise.

Mouth's refusal to don the 'I', like the old woman's quest, in *Rockaby*, for another 'with famished eyes/like hers',[21] moreover, reveals not only the insufficient appropriation of the transcendental consciousness in the first-person pronoun, but that inability of consciousness to conceptualise itself in its totality of which we spoke a moment ago. It is precisely the impossibility of any complete self-perception either as an individual or as an anonymous presence—the impossibility, in other words, of a reflexive objectifying self-consciousness in which one's status as a communicative being in a social situation is utterly externalised—that leads the old woman, like Mouth, both to continue seeking recognition of herself in the Other—hence 'More'—and to glimpse, intermittently, her individuality: 'Whom else' she persists, and not so ironically, in asking. Thus it is at that very moment when the old maid abandons her quest of the Other, saying to herself 'no/done with that', that time stops, the rocker is told to 'rock her off' and perception—in the twice repeated line: 'Stop her eyes'[22]—ceases, putting an end to that tension between anonymity and individuality that is the *sine qua non* of all transcendental experience *and* an end to the language of the play as the metaphoric correlate of intentional projection.

III

A clue to the understanding of Beckett's plays in terms of the unveiling of the self in the dialectic of its anonymous and individualising relation to the world is provided by Butler's reminder that '*all* metaphysical and ontological language is metaphorical and, to that extent, "not true"'.[23] Such language overlaps poetic or narrative discourse, Butler explains, in its recourse to analogy for articulation. Heidegger's concept of '*Geworfenheim*' ('Throwness') serves as an example: 'There is no question but that this is a metaphor: Heidegger does not intend us to conceive a man as "thrown" into Being literally'.[24] Similarly, '. . . when the actor in *Act Without Words I* is literally flung onto the stage we automatically grope for the meaning of that flinging in just the same way as we try to seize the philosopher's concept'.[25]

If we consider the concept of metaphor in the light of Paul Ricoeur's investigations into its function in *La Metaphore Vive*, and also in the light of philosopher-critic Jacques Garelli's analysis, in *Le Recel et la Dispersion*, of the poetic *Aufhebung*—the process of dialectical negation and constitution through which the world is negated in its limited individuality, preserved in its essential being and elevated, in the imagistic or metaphoric use of language, to a higher reality, a 'surreality'—we see that it is precisely in the overlapping of the literal with the poetic in the metaphorical functioning of both ontological and creative discourse that the autoconstitutional and self-reflective nature of the fiction—*which is that metaphor*—resides. For Garelli, in fact, the 'surreal' or poetic constitution of a fictive universe is dependent on this paradox of self-reflection:

Il y a un paradoxe de l'activité poétique qui est la mesure de sa condition. Ouverture sur le monde, le poème est, dans l'acte du dévoilement, cela même qui est dévoilé. Regard, il se fait voir. Lumière, il s'éclaire. Révélateur, il ne révèle qu'en étant lui-meme révélé. Le secret du langage poétique, le surgissement sauvage de son dire dans la gorge, sa distribution rythmique et sonore par l'acte de lecture, résident dans la structure de cette ambiguité. En d'autres termes, *naturata et naturans*, l'oeuvre poétique rend présent ce qui ouvre une présence.[26]

[There is a paradox of poetic activity which is the measure of its very condition. Opening onto the world, the poem, in the act of unveiling, is that which is unveiled. Looking, it makes itself seen. Enlightening, it illuminates itself. Revealing, it reveals only in being itself revealed. The secret of poetic language, the turbulent arising of its expression from within the throat, its rhythmic and sonorous distribution through the act of reading, all reside within the structure of this ambiguity. In other words, *naturata and naturans*, the poetic work makes present that which opens onto a presence.]

Investigated as a metaphorical correlate of an intentionalising consciousness, in terms, therefore, of the autoconstitutional and self-reflective functioning of the textual language, *Not I* may be said to function as a dramatic narrative insofar as it is a *textual re-doubling*, a reflection of nothing other than its *own process of revelation*.

Further insight into this process might be gleaned from the congruence of narrative and metanarrative that is achieved in *Not I* within the temporalisation of the fictional language. The endless repetition of Mouth's tale of that April morning implies not a temporality conceived as a passage from past to present, and from present to future, but rather an existential or lived term, a temporality conceived as an eternal present, to that extent that Mouth's tale is, essentially, the actuality of Beckett's drama. This is to say that the 'then' of Mouth's narration is contemporaneous with the 'now' of her metanarration provoking a deliberate confusion of text with reality that Enoch Brater has described as follows:

> Although *Not I* appears to be 'about' Mouth, not eye (co-starring Auditor as ear), the piece is perhaps a far more subtle vehicle that this unruly trinity would imply. Although Mouth speaks, Auditor hears, and audience sees, Beckett creates for his audience a visual and aural stimulus closely approximating the 'matter' of the monologue itself. The 'buzzing' in the ear is in fact the strange buzzing in our ears; the spotlight on Mouth becomes the 'ray or beam' we ourselves see . . .[27]

It is in this perspective that Mouth's intermittent screams, moreover, are to be interpreted, screams which ironically interrupt the only quasi-historical account of her inability, on that April morning, to 'make the sound . . . not any sound . . . so sound of any kind . . . no screaming for help for example . . . should she *feel*'—which we might oppose to the more appropriate or expected past: have felt—'so inclined'.[28]

We are prohibited from further analysis here of those textual structures in Beckett's work that have been outlined by Ricoeur, Garelli and others in terms of the intentional, temporal and surrealising dimensions of all art. A more extensive investigation of the significance of a phenomenological ontology and, specifically, of Butler's notion of 'ontological parable' for the understanding of anonymity and individuality in Beckett would, however, uncover a variety of questions pertinent to both the thematisation of ontology and ontological functioning of Beckett's language.

Among the more significant would no doubt be the relevance of gender identity, and its counterpart, sexual indeterminacy, to a phenomenological hermeneutics. Gender identity in Beckett has already lent itself to fruitful inquiry in the context of recent feminist criticism and the monologues of *Not I* and *Rockaby* have been considered as displaying a distinctly female discourse supporting the designation of the two primary personages as women. In situating the question of gender identity on the order of intentionality, as opposed once again to that of representation in these two plays is more fundamentally *arbitrary* for the anonymity of the ontological structures of Being-in-the-World that Beckett's entire fictional corpus embodies, and their relation to the process of individuation, the progressive formation of self-awareness, might indeed be shown to negate any valorization of gender determination whatsoever—this, however, in a distinctly humanising (rather than dehumanising) perspective. It is along these lines, perhaps, that clues might be found to the playwright's specification that the Auditor in *Not I*, like the narrator of *Enough*, be of undetermined gender. Does Beckett not appear to conceive of a language *preceding* gender appropriation, a primary and originary language which would, in its freedom from the political and ideological functioning of a masculine or feminine discourse, approximate the language of Being to which Heidegger wished us all to attend? When all is said and done, has not language been reduced by Beckett to the utterance of some essential and unequivocal phenomenon—that exemplified by two identical cries 'switching on and off strictly synchronized light and breath'?[29]

WALKING AND ROCKING: RITUAL ACTS IN *FOOTFALLS* AND *ROCKABY*

MARY A. DOLL

In *Footfalls* (1976) and *Rockaby* (1981) walking and rocking provide yet another link between two similar plays. Both plays feature a woman and her voice. In both, the voice rather than the woman before our eyes, compels interest and attention. In both, bodies seem ghostly. May, in *Footfalls* for instance, is described in the stage directions as having '*Dishevelled grey hair, worn grey wrap hiding feet, trailing*', while in *Rockaby*, Woman is described as '*Prematurely old. Unkempt grey hair. Huge eyes in white expressionless face*'.[1] These characters also share a remarkable similarity to Beckett's plays of the same years that involve male characters interacting with male voices (*That Time*, 1976, and *Ohio Impromptu*, 1981). In both sets of plays the main characters appear on stage strangely—'not there', 'slightly off centre'. The characters, not centred literally, are removed also spiritually and psychically from the core of being.

And yet it is precisely this distance, felt deeply, that marks a dramatic intensity of the plays. Split off from their inner core, their souls, the characters must listen, listen, to a voice. The voice torments with memories of failed connections, painful desires. It intrudes as from below. The characters are capable neither of altering its presence nor of fathoming its message. Strangely, however, the voice seems to provide nourishment. It is as if the characters *need* voice to give them substance; as if, *without* the voice, their bodies are but urns.

Clearly, Beckett turns upside down the Aristotelian notion of 'character', complete in body, capable with speech, conquering time with action. Indeed, Beckett's characters, particularly the recent ones, seem less whole in body than even Watt (1970) or Winnie (1961). May not only has a poor arm, a poor head, and a poor mind, she also has a poor appetite. *Rockaby*'s Woman, robbed of named identity, neither acts nor talks. Her only utterance is the word 'More', which, as Billie Whitelaw pronounces it, sounds like 'maw', to suggest a need for nourishment. These people *appear* famished, because they *are*. They are starved for soul. Feeling their psychic voids as a deep inner hunger, they are reduced to minimal motion: walking, rocking.

Such motions of back and forth, up and down, however, are the very stuff of ritual, which is drama through and through. According to Mircea Eliade, ceaseless repetitive acts (like walking and rocking) can have the effect of making sacred that which is profane. Inside 'sacred space', time can be reversed. A person performing ritual acts can transform time backwards; she can meet the inhabitants of an older cosmos: voices, ghosts, souls long dead.[2] There, is no time, the time of the gods, the soul lives eternally. In exercising basic steps and repeated gestures, the women of Beckett's recent plays can thus be considered as initiates, who seek connection with forces that feed the soul.

I am interested in two old ideas as they relate to Beckett's recent work. One old idea is the Orphic doctrine, according to which the soul was believed to occupy a buried space within the body—buried as in a prison.[3] The second old idea, related to the first, is Plato's pun that the body (soma) is a tomb (sēma).[4] The word sēma means 'sign from heaven, omen, portent', and then, 'any sign, like a signal to begin battle', and finally, 'the marker, or sign, indicating a grave'. These ideas invert normal perception, turn inside out such fundamental categories as 'body', 'soul', 'life', 'death'. A person wracked with despair, accordingly signals to the outer world that a battle with the soul is being waged. The body in pain or agony portends an 'untombing' process. This world and all its concerns become mere shadow, without material substance, because an Other world is forcing itself upon awareness. For the initiate, this experience feels like a death; the wracked person feels inside the land of dead souls. Murray Stein, in his book on radical or liminal stages of life, explains the psychological import of such experience:

> Orphism, as a religion of liminality, shows how palpable the soul becomes during liminality, and as the sense of psychic reality increases, the sense of the material world's importance declines. . . . A person in liminality has 'dropped out', 'gone away', to 'another place', 'disappeared' into social and psychological invisibility. Here a radical sort of introversion and immersion in the unconscious has taken place and the inner world consequently becomes more real and charged with energy than the outer adaptive context.[5]

Even as early as *Murphy* (1938) Beckett was playing in fiction with a dynamic between body and nonbody (or 'mind' as he called it then). 'Murphy's mind', he wrote, 'pictured itself as a large hollow sphere, hermetically closed to the universe without'.[6] The mind, 'bodytight', (p. 109), contained three zones of light, half light, and dark, 'each with its speciality' (p. 111). Because this inner universe was so vast and complicated and interesting, it became a space that both Murphy and Celia sought actively by tying themselves into their rocking chair. The inactions of body were more than made up for by the actions of mind.

In his recent plays Beckett shifts from the word 'mind' to the word 'voice', putting a different, more Orphic quality on the reality of the inner universe. Voice has new potency, capable of interrupting the natural rhythms of sleep or death. By forcing its claim on the body, voice speaks of 'it all', the pain of 'it all', 'revolving' in the mind. Yet paradoxically the pain voice brings allays the pain of body, which is also wracked. And body, in pain, opens a window on the soul.

Through body, ceremonies of deepest significance are given form.[7] In his work on ritual Mircea Eliade identifies three steps whereby body-acts become transformative processes. These correspond strikingly with Beckett's recent plays, in which women appear—for all the world—like sleepwalkers or half-dead people. Their ghostliness, however, serves as a sign that significant inner action with the soul is in process. Ritualistically, the women must 'fall' from flesh and all that flesh demands if they are to meet with the invisible factors of an Other world. In a sense, they must become the ghosts they seem. Back and forth, up and down body actions, thus, satisfy three conditions of ritual. One, the acts create a threshold, whereby a difference between two time modalities is felt not physiologically, but sacramentally. Two, the acts inaugurate body into a nocturnal regime, wherein souls acquire reality. And three, ritual body-acts force a recognition, or knowing-again, of the doubleness of all reality, whereby subjects and objects are harnessed, as horses to a rack.[8] Let us then see how Eliade's conditions apply to the Beckettian situation, wherein body no matter how ghostly—or perhaps because of the ghost —shows forth the soul.

In both *Footfalls* and *Rockaby* a threshold between two modes of reality is situated in the speaker's particular time-span on earth. May, in the first play, is in her forties (p. 44)—although her appearance would suggest she is older, or without age. She is, in other words, at the time of midlife crisis when body is midway through its journey in life, a stage of liminality. The soul, normally entombed during periods of light and wakefulness, begins to stir. As Murray Stein puts it:

What seems to come to fuller consciousness during midlife liminality is . . . an awareness of *psyche*, . . . the soul that is otherwise dormant and invisible in the bright light of waking consciousness. Consciousness of soul, or soul-consciousness, seems to be the chief product of midlife liminality (p. 126).

Stein goes on to describe midlife journey as ghostly:

The journeyers, or floaters, feel ghostlike, even to themselves. . . . 'Ghost' is equivalent to 'soul', and in liminality the soul is awakened and released . . . and a person . . . ventures into psychological regions that are otherwise unknown, inaccessible, or forbidden (p. 136).

May in her forties is, nevertheless, in the very springtime of psychic life.

Rockaby's Woman is at an opposite season of time. Yet, in her winter, she too goes to and fro. End-of-life, another critical moment, is, importantly, another threshold, when every loss signifies more (Stein, p. 47). Especially during life's winter journey, soul expresses its need to 'get itself born' through such body holes as eyes, ears, or mouth. Woman's only utterance—the single word 'more'—should be heard as a mantra at the threshold, inviting soul to detach itself from bodied entombment.

Threshold awareness is also signalled in these two plays by the difficulty both women have in either making themselves understood or in establishing human relationship. 'What do you mean?' . . .'What can you possibly mean?' This is the question Voice asks of May as Voice tries to tell May's story. The question synchronises with May's nightwalking. It is a question an audience would want to pose as well: what does it mean, this walking around in circles? All we can gather is that May's nightwalking, begun when she was a child, is an attempt to somehow compensate for a felt insufficiency:

Till one night while still little more than a child, she called her mother and said, Mother, this is not enough. The mother: Not enough? May—the child's given name—May: Not enough. The mother: What do you mean, May, not enough, what can you possibly mean, May, not enough? (p. 45)

In May's story, called 'sequel', (a pun for 'seek well', Beckett tells us [9]), negative communication is the theme. The story, about a mother and daughter at supper, is literally a 'night story', about the nocturnal regime. Old Mrs. Winter late one autumn evening sits down to supper with her daughter Amy (anagram for May). Neither of them appears well. A question is asked about the Evensong service.

Was there, the mother asks, anything strange about it? Amy observed nothing strange. Perhaps, Mrs. Winter says, it was just my fancy:

Mrs. W: You yourself observed nothing . . . strange?
Amy: No, Mother, I myself did not, to put it mildly.
Mrs. W: What do you mean, Amy, to put it mildly.
Amy: I mean, Mother, that to say I observed nothing. . . strange is indeed to put it mildly. For I observed nothing of any kind, strange or otherwise. I saw nothing, heard nothing, of any kind. I was not there (p. 48).

This tale of chilling non-understanding and dead-end communication has at its middle the daughter's phrase 'Just what exactly, Mother, did you perhaps fancy it was?' 'Meaning', juxtaposed with 'fancy', or fantasy, suggests that at the centre of a bare-bones world, in the heart of winter's night, fancy is only a 'perhaps'—not entirely 'there'.

But that fancy, or fantasy, can emerge at all is a triumph. For these ghostly figures fantasy is food. Calling her story a 'semblance', May knows it tells of an experience only half understood: ill seen, ill said. Even so, in telling it, she is nourished, for the words seem to feed her soul. Beckett's poetics compare here with Plato's *Phaedrus*, in which the soul is pictured as imprisoned in a rack between two unruly steeds. Confounded and confused, the soul is denied full understanding and must 'feed upon the food of semblance'.[10] Invisible presences, or semblances, thus become the substance for the psyche, 'racked' in confusion with the body.

A similar situation is seen with Woman in *Rockaby*, who, also on the edge of all possible relationship, needs invisible semblances to feed her soul. Here the difficulty is not within relationship, Mother with Daughter, but within the species itself. Woman, simply, can find no other face, no other pair of eyes, no other body, to validate her existence. Her search is pathetically modest. All she seeks is 'one blind up', one other window open, where one 'a little like' herself can mirror back to her, herself: some tiny validation that she exists. At the window threshold, however, there is no Other. It now becomes clear that if she *is* to find an Other, the semblance of soul in the world, she must look beyond subjects, to objects. Perhaps there, in objects, she will find the 'more' that she seeks.

'Being at the threshold' thus involves body-use in a radical or ritual way. Body must be used bodily to feel, not just to know, soul. Such attachment to body is totally different from *Happy Days*, for instance, when Winnie, stuck in the ground, is grounded in imagination. Grounded reality is indicated by Winnie's corpulence. Beckett describes her too-substantial flesh as 'well preserved, plump', with 'big bosom' (p. 7). That she is 'about fifty' indicated that she, unlike May, is beyond midlife and the particular liminal consciousness that midlife brings. Grounded literal reality is also mirrored back to Winnie by Shower or Cooker's coarseness. When coming across her body 'stuck up to her diddies in the bleeding ground', he asks, '. . . What does it mean? . . . What's it meant to mean?' (p. 43). Meaning in such a surface world can only be apprehended crudely. Far from the ghostly search that haunts May and Woman, the question of meaning in the bright light of *Happy Days* does not penetrate soul.

The two women in *Footfalls* and *Rockaby* share a second ritual body-act: the making of space for soul. Because they are *out* of the centre, they must make sacred the *off*-centre place in which they find themselves, circumscribing it until More can come forth. In *Footfalls* space is created by the act of walking, whereby May not only feels her feet, she also hears them, however faint they fall. This recalls Gogo in *Waiting for Godot*, whose difficulty with his feet suggests a discomfort with surface reality, a yearning for dream, and a desire to touch what Katherine Burkman calls 'negative epiphany'.[11] Reportedly, when Beckett was asked the meaning of the word 'godot' he said it came from the slang for *boot* in French—*godillot, godasse*—because feet play such a prominent part.[12] The pacing of feet literally defines limits and creates space, through which the depth dimension can be felt. In *Rockaby* space is created with the voice in spoken rhythms that set off metrical feet. Metaphors scribed and circumscribed again and again acquire deeper and deeper meanings that turn truth to fancy and fancy into truth. Both women thus create space for soul: one physically, with feet; the other poetically, with voice.

May creates space beyond the centre by pacing nine steps and making left-turn circles. Elsewhere I have compared May's left-turn circles with the Eleusinian Mystery rites that imitated Demeter's grieving.[13] By moving counter-clockwise, away from the centre, in the wrong direction, Eleusinian initiates performed grief ceremonies intended to transform raw feeling. May's deliberate pacing to the left establishes just such a connection with the sinister, or left, side of experience, holistic in an uncentred way. In addition, the number nine, with its multiples of three—uneven numbers all—serves as an invocation to enter a nocturnal realm where opposites cannot be diametrically pitted.

May draws her circle in nine steps, in a sequence Beckett makes specific:

Pacing: starting with right foot (r) from right (R) to left (L).
with left foot (l) from L to R.
Turn: rightabout at L. leftabout at R.
Steps: clearly audible tread (p.42).

Needing to hear, not simply to move, her feet, May must feel the space she is creating as coming to her from underneath. She must feel the underworld.

A similar attention to sensing the space one is creating is seen in *Rockaby*, when Woman's voice paces itself through nine uneven sequences. Like May's feet, Woman's voice turns back on itself at a precise point in the narration, prohibiting story from getting beyond itself, forcing images to turn and return until they become like spokes of a wheel.

The phrase that signals voice's turn, repeated nine times, is 'all eyes/all sides', each turning seeming to locate the eyes progressively lower, until the organ of seeing becomes no longer located in the head but in some lower region of bodily awareness—the feet, perhaps. The first three times the voice turns on the phrase 'going to and fro/ all eyes/ all sides' (pp.9, 10); the fourth time the pattern breaks to 'going to and fro/ all eyes like herself/ all sides' (p. 10). Times five through eight the turning phrase is simplified to 'all eyes/ all sides', while the ninth and final turn of phrase is 'she so long all eyes/ famished eyes/ all sides' (p. 19). Each turning of the text, no matter which variation, contains the phrase 'high and low', following the refrain 'all eyes/ all sides', to suggest a synchronistic movement both of eyes searching high and low and of chair rocking high and low. The effect is wonderfully curious, for although Woman's eyes remain unblinking according to Beckett's directions (p. 22), Voice tells us they are constantly active; and although the chair is inanimate, it seems to comfort with its encircling arms.

In *Cosmos and History*, Mircea Eliade stresses a difference between archaic and modern experience that pertains to the paradoxes Beckett's Woman constantly display. Archaic experience is, Eliade tells us, suffused with Cosmos and with the rhythms of the Cosmos. Modern experience, on the other hand, connects only with history. Eliade writes:

It is useless to search archaic languages for the terms so laboriously created by the great philosophical traditions; there is every likelihood that such words as 'being', 'nonbeing', 'real', 'unreal', 'becoming', 'illusory', are not to be found in the language of the Australians or of the ancient Mesopotamians. But if the word is lacking, the *thing* is present; only it is 'said'—that is, revealed in a coherent fashion—through symbols and myths.[14]

As a third 'moment' of ritual expression in Beckett's recent plays, a valuing of the *thing* is seen. Objects rather than subjects contain the More; objects, indeed, take the place of language, showing forth silently yet poetically the doubleness of all reality.

Beckett's interest in objective reality and in an object-centred art probably began with his interest in painting, with his admiration of the works of Jack B. Yeats, Henri Hayden, and the Dutch brothers Geer and Bram van Velde. On their canvases, a viewer's eyes were assaulted with strange objects that seemed to take on a reality of their own. In praising this new object-centred art, Beckett wrote, in 1934, of the marvellous way objects had revealing layers of being: by seeing objects, he wrote, we can begin to see again ourselves—as complex multiplicities.[15] Earlier in 1931, in a more famous explication (*Proust*), Beckett had begun to formulate his theory of the object 'isolated and inexplicable' and therefore 'a source of enchantment'.[16] When language fails to communicate and when words no longer 'speak', then meaning must be embodied in other forms: body-acts, theatre-images, objects.[17]

This turning to objects as source of meaning is evident in Beckett's work throughout his career. From Lucky's bones and the tree in *Godot*;from Winnie's bag; from Krapp's tape; from Molloy's stones: objects become touchstones of true existential meaning for starved Beckettian souls. In *Company*, the work that many consider Beckett's autobiography, selfhood is *defined* by objects which assume an iconic power of 'semblance'.[18] By simply gazing at a blade of grass or observing the shape of a buttonhook, the narrator of *Company* glimpses an Other dimension, apart from familiar time and place. In that brief glimpsing, another world is conveyed; for in the object, so much More is contained than that which can be said.[19]

Rockaby's Woman is case in point. The subjects in her world have deserted her. Left by herself in her rocking chair, all she seeks is one other, a little like herself. But this 'one' does not appear. The Other creature, somewhere there, behind windows, never opens the blinds. Day after day, at her window, Woman looks for a face in the pane—as does the generic character 'A' in *That Time*, also character 'B', also character 'C': each a One, searching for validity in the object world of museums, slabs, ruins. Beckett implies that because 'company' *cannot* be found with subjects, objects at least make the solitary condition clear. This truth is comfort of a kind.

Woman's object-companions are windows and chairs. The windows, blinded, do not provide eyes to the soul but rather mirror back a stark and barren truth: 'a blind up/like hers/ a little like/ one blind up no more' (p. 16). Facing other windows, Woman faces only blindsightedness, like her own; other panes, like her own pains; 'behind the pane/ another living soul' (p. 16). Beckett suggests that only in pain can soul be seen, as through a glass, clearly. Yet, for Woman, it is time she stopped searching: the 'only' windows of *Rockaby*, like the 'perhaps' fancy of *Footfalls*, yields nothing—no other living soul.

Chair, on the other hand, offers something more. Nestled inside her rocking chair, knowing it as her only reality, Woman spends her days rocking to and fro, dressed in 'best black' (p. 17). As in the French *chair* for flesh or *pain* for bread, the object world mirrors back dimensions of the human condition, wherein suffering is the very stuff, or staff, of life. Chair, indeed, rocks with the voice, as if to imply a new language: that of a rocking voice speaking in fragments rather than lines. The chairs arms communicate embrace—'*rounded curving arms to suggest embrace*' the stage directions say (p. 22)—so that comfort denied by subjects is given freely by objects.

But objective reality in Beckett is not the opposite of subjective reality, not more kind. In making her left-turn circles, May wheels up and down, up and down, 'like moon through passing . . . rack' (p. 47). The word 'rack' signifies, first, a framework or stand for the display of articles; second, a toothed bar that meshes with another toothed bar, such as a pinion or gearwheel; third, a framelike instrument of torture. Other meanings of 'rack' relate familiar Beckettian themes with certain Platonic undertones: namely, a) either of two gaits of horses, b) a thin mass of wind-driven clouds, c) destruction—as in rack and ruin, d) to drain from the dregs, as wine or cider, and e) a wholesale rib cut of lamb between the shoulder and the loin. Rack, thus, as object, conveys More than, say, wheel. Not only does it reduce to a pulp, grind, or mesh; it also does these things in a way that feels like a torture. Being 'wracked' with pain suggests this connotation, just as Plato's 'racked' soul struggles in opposite direction. To be 'racked', thus, is to be going forward while being pulled backwards; it is to be drawn and quartered.

All the various ideas of these two plays come together to bear upon a single word, key object for all subjects. 'Rack', as the frame upon which other images hang, describes May's wheeling body-act, wherein her torture may be encircled. 'Rack' also describes May's body, which, like hanging meat—shoulder, or loin—appears bloodless. Equally, Woman's rocking describes *her* rack, pinioned to its spot. Yet, *except* for the doubts that cloud them, Beckett's characters would be empty vessels, mere urns.[20] Wracked feelings give substance. Fleeting moments of memory pass through May, 'like moon through passing . . . rack'. Fleeting glimpses, 'one blind up', give Woman a wisp of hope. Racks, thus, are the rocks on which Being is founded.

Perhaps something of a Platonic pun runs through these later works of Beckett. The only difference, after all, between body (soma) and tomb (sēma) is a shift in vowels. Similarly, the only difference between rack and rock is the vowel shift. Such shifts soften meaning, make it more subject to the query 'What exactly do you mean?' But as Beckett's women show us, meaning no longer lodges itself firmly in single words, single concepts, exact definitions. Meaning, rather, hovers like a ghost, in images, actions, objects, and despairing hopes. Among *these* layers lie hidden, other worlds.

BECKETT'S OTHER TRILOGY: *NOT I*, *FOOTFALLS*, AND *ROCKABY*

R. THOMAS SIMONE

One of the most intriguing and significant aspects of Beckett's dramatic work of the last fifteen years has been his meditation on the image of women through his work with the British actress Billie Whitelaw. Beckett was fascinated by the quality of Whitelaw's voice in the 1964 Royal Court production of *Play*, and he apparently determined to write 'a play' for her in the future.[1] According to Ruby Cohn, 'Beckett vividly remembered, as he wrote . . ., that Whitelaw was "so remarkable in *Play* and brilliant vocally."'[2] The work that emerged was *Not I* of 1972, but we know that Beckett's response to Whitelaw was not limited to the writing of that one play. Beckett continued throughout the 1970s to produce other works specifically for Whitelaw, *Footfalls* and *Rockaby*, and he worked with her intensively on three landmark productions, the British premiere of *Not I* in 1973, the world premiere of *Footfalls* in 1976, and the revival of *Happy Days* in 1979—all at the Royal Court Theatre. While Beckett was not announced as the director of the Royal Court *Not I*, he exerted authoritative control on the production during rehearsals. The 1979 production of *Happy Days*, so Beckett claimed, was to be his farewell to direction in the theatre. He has worked, however, on a few other productions since that time, and he was present in 1982 at rehearsals for the National Theatre of Britain *Rockaby* that was directed by the late Alan Schneider, and Beckett presumably had a direct effect on that production.[3] Thus, Beckett's work with Whitelaw has included both the writing of plays for her and the expression of his directorial influence on the production of these works.[4]

While the figures of women appear, of course, in many other Beckett plays—we may think of Maddie Rooney in the radio play *All That Fall* (1956) or of Nell in *Endgame* (1958) or the two women in *Play* (1964)—he attains his most sustained and provocative presentation of the place of women and 'woman' in the Beckettian dramatic universe in *Happy Days* and in the Whitelaw trilogy. What I call, at times, for the sake of brevity, 'the Whitelaw trilogy', does not have the formal and official unity of the fiction trilogy, but it does have a unity of dramatic inspiration and initial presentation. Further, these plays represent Beckett's extension of certain images established in *Happy Days* and a most moving dramatisation of the human dilemma as he has understood it in his recent work. The *Happy Days* production of 1979 drew the link between the Whitelaw trilogy and the earlier play, but it also helped to show that the trilogy existed separately as a stylistic and dramatic continuity. James Knowlson's comment on the make-up in Act 2 of the Royal Court/*Happy Days* production underscores this link: 'the make-up of Act II was deathly pale, as the same actress's had been in *Footfalls*'[5]. While the Winnie of the Beckett/Whitelaw Act I is radically different in presentation from the women of the trilogy, the Winnie of Act II prefigures them. The plays that Beckett has written since *Rockaby*, such as *Ohio Impromptu* (1981), *Catastrophe* (1982), and *What Where* (1983), turn from central female figures back to a world that is dominated by male imagery and by a more abstract kind of drama. For the moment, then, Beckett seems to have concluded this sequence of plays that focus on central female figures and which were written specifically with Billie Whitelaw in mind.[6]

Beckett's major achievement in these three plays, in addition to his presentation of a range of material centred on women, is the attainment of a new kind of drama. Martin Esslin considers that *Footfalls* marks a 'radically different type of drama, almost of new art-form'. He continues to define this new type of drama as one 'where it is quite impossible to make sense of the words, what remains is a pure image, the poetical metaphor concretised into a picture, a moving and sounding picture, but essentially a picture nevertheless'.[7] Where Esslin sees this new drama of concretised image beginning in *Footfalls*, I believe we can see traces of such visionary drama in earlier Beckett plays, and especially in *Not I*. In *Not I* the unstoppable stream of broken phrases, as the continual testament of the Mouth, becomes itself the image of the suffering and the separation of self from language. In the television version, which Beckett himself is reported to have preferred over the stage version, the dominant image of the mouth attains that newly intensified status of image that overwhelms narrative continuity. Beckett wrote to Jessica Tandy about *Not I* in terms that suggest that he was aware of working on this new kind of drama already in 1972.

I am not unduly concerned with intelligibility. I hope the piece may work on the nerves of the audience, not on its intellect.[8]

The image and impact of *Not I* overwhelm the critical faculty in its attempt to explain this disturbing play. I would agree with Mr. Esslin that *That Time* (1975) did not attain the level of this new type of drama, at least in its premiere production, but I find that the Whitelaw plays all partake of Beckett's distillation of stage image and drama into a new and remarkable unity.

While we continue to marvel at the fertility of Beckett's imagination in so many works and forms, I would like to claim a particular place in his late work for this group of plays—*Not I*, *Footfalls*, and *Rockaby*. Here we discover Beckett's unparalleled powers of dramatic concentration, but also a richer imagery through the figures of the women in these plays. The themes of sexuality, the body, the dissociation of mind from self, and the inability of language to reveal adequate meaning are all taken to new levels in these three works. Further, Beckett seems to have entered in these three plays into a new form of drama that both advances his craft as playwright and increases the emotional and artistic effect of the work.

Although Beckett's direction of Whitelaw in *Happy Days* came late during the period of these encounters, it was instructive because of the contrast in stage presentation between the figure of Winnie, especially in Act I, and those of the other women in the Whitelaw trilogy. The stage image of the women figures in *Not I*, *Footfalls*, and *Rockaby* share the aspect of the exhaustion of the traditional aspects of the feminine in Beckett's world. Where *Endgame* or *Krapp's Last Tape* shows the exhaustion of existence in strongly male terms, *Footfalls*, for example, concentrates on a woman arrested in her abstraction from nature as a woman. May's disappearance from her own narrative of Amy and Old Mrs. Winter and her physical disappearance from the play in the crucial fourth scene, where we see only the still fainter path of light, become the epitome of the failure of the meaning of existence in Beckett's late plays.

In *Not I* we have the reduction of the image of the woman in the play to the Mouth that we see illuminated on stage. In the narrative of the Mouth the woman in her story is 'an old hag already'(p. 220), 'seventy . . . coming up on . . . good God . . . coming up to seventy' (p. 216).[9] The Mouth and the woman in her story, who is, we gather, the self-fictionalization of the speaker in old age and deprivation, exist in potent opposition as the title of the play suggest. However, the image of the mouth—particularly in Bill Morton's BBC television version—suggests both an erotic power and an animal energy that go far beyond the external narrative idea of an old hag. Thus, while the narrative of Mouth dwells on abandonment in childhood and abstraction from the world in old age, the visual effect of the play is intensely emotional and erotic. The image of the Mouth with almost constant movement, the saliva, teeth, tongue, and lips, the suggestion not just of mouth but of orifice—remains as a disturbing image for the viewer. The effect is of the most extreme rejection of presence in time and in body by the voice, but paradoxically for the viewer of an almost unbearable *presence* of suffering and immediacy of the physical. Surely there are few works by any author that show such unmediated presence. It may have been this very immediacy that made the role of the Mouth so overwhelming for Whitelaw, who, after the premiere production and the taping of the television version, has refused to go through the difficulty of acting *Not I* again.

May of *Footfalls*, who is apparently forty-five, according to the dialogue of the first tableau, appears as a grey 'tangle of tatters'. Here again the fraught figure of Whitelaw, dressed in a grey web of a dress with tensed and crossed arms, was unforgettable. The contrast between Whitelaw-May of 1976 and the Act I Whitelaw-Winnie of 1979 was stunning. Where Beckett had her Winnie appear as a siren, her May was a figure of grey intensity and anger against the earth as she continued to 'revolve it all in her poor mind'. The sense of youth and the feminine swallowed up by decay and decrepitude of existence is overwhelming in *Footfalls*. The woman of *Rockaby*, who seems almost to be a continuation of May, is dressed in the black sequined dress and hat of the mother, and in that costume the rocked woman embodies the images of mother and daughter while at the same time rejecting the life that has given those images. The grey and pacing May of *Footfalls* and the black sequined, rocking woman of *Rockaby* form a set of images that mirror one another suggestively. In this as in many other aspects, the women of these three plays seem to have a shared family existence that parallels the interrelationships of the narrators of the fiction trilogy.

As a sequence of dramatic visions, these three plays present the metamorphosis of images of women and a striking progression of tempo and tone. This progression was heightened by the intercalated production of *Happy Days* between *Footfalls* of 1976 and *Rockaby* of 1980. In the *Happy Days* of 1979, Beckett very particularly played upon the physical attractiveness of Whitelaw. The initial stage direction of *Happy Days* has Winnie, embedded to her waist in the mound in Act I, where she is described as being '[a]bout fifty, well preserved, blond for preference, plump, arms and shoulders bare, low bodice, big bosom, pearl necklet'.[10] Where most Winnies, such as Peggy Ashcroft and Irene Worth, look rather matronly, Beckett made

Whitelaw's Winnie into a siren, with black, low cut gown, haunting eyes, exaggerated lipstick. We could see in this production, along with the initial despair under Winnie's cheerfulness, a woman, who while not any longer young, still manifests a powerful erotic dimension.

In the Beckett *Happy Days* at the Royal Court, the advance of the mound of earth became both the inevitable engulfing of the person by cosmos and the extreme frustration of the sexual and the female body in Winnie. In retrospect, the vision of *Not I* with the Mouth as the presentation of a woman shows a strongly erotic and animal force. The emphasis on the orifice of the Mouth and suggestions of a vagina was all the more striking in the television version of *Not I*. Beckett's approval of this imaging, as reported by Ruby Cohn among others, carried over into a deletion of the Auditor from Beckett's first French production.[11] While *Not I* seems at one level to be an extension of the masking of the body begun in *Happy Days*, the Mouth actually emphasizes the energy, allure, and the danger of the body. As Paul Lawley has suggested, it is the very absence of the body in the stage picture that calls attention to and renovates the cliches of the body and references to the body throughout the Mouth's narrative.[12] While the antinomy between narrator and character is sustained and forms the core of the spoken drama, the opposition of shapeless auditor and the human body reduced to a mouth is intensified on television through the image of the mouth and the absence of the rest of the body. Perhaps, also, with the absence of the actor through the electronic medium, the viewer effectively absorbs the role of the auditor and even becomes the sympathetic and threatened body.

Within the context of Whitelaw's siren presentation of Winnie, the women of *Not I*, *Footfalls*, and *Rockaby* can be seen as both physically and emotionally in revolt against the earth. In *Footfalls* we see May 'revolving it all' in her mind and in her pacing of the path of light, and her intensity of pacing and denying persists into the mutely eloquent final tableau of the path of light. This is a masterstroke of Beckett's, presenting most completely his meditation on presence and absence in his drama. May's rejection of the idea of her birth and her anger against this unresponsive world lead to her deletion of her self in scene three from her narrative of Amy and Old Mrs. Winter. Her disappearance from the stage and the last fade up and out of the path of light express both the rejection of life and the persistence of vision. The woman on stage in *Rockaby* exists in her imitation of her mother as a woman in black gown and hat. Where May is dressed in a grey tangle of tatters, the rocking woman wears an antiquated sequined black dress, both imitating her mother and waiting for death. she exists as she *is* rocked, as she summons 'more' from her own thoughts and her own life, as she is drawn down into the rocker towards her death. The rejection of the earth is more veiled in *Rockaby* than in *Not I* and *Footfalls*, but it springs out at us as the mood of acquiescence alternates with the desire for more, and the final mood is one of death and the rejection of life.

done with that
the rocker
whose arms at last
saying to the rocker
rock her off
stop her eyes
fuck life
stop her eyes
rock her off (p. 282)

As in *Not I*, the outer image of stasis, withdrawal, and resignation, only masks an intensity of suffering and anger against existence. Granted that the tone of *Rockaby* is elegiac, the voice betrays an anger that has never been extinguished. While we see the images of the woman, her mother, the rocker, and mother earth, the woman through her voice declares her rejection of what May calls 'it all'.

All three plays in the Whitelaw trilogy achieve a particular emotional power through dramatic presentation and in dramatic narrative of female images. In this they share with *Happy Days* in a range of associations with the female body, with female sexuality, and particularly with the associations of birth and its frustration. As the speaker of *A Piece of Monologue* begins in a masculine mode, 'Birth was the death of him' (p. 265). But, of course, here we have images of an actress miming the parts of women and enacting speech, birth and its rejection, and the acceptance of death in the mother rocker. The theme of the inefficacy of birth haunts Beckett's plays from *Godot* on. Vladimir's reverie on birth and death is the central passage: 'Astride of a grave and difficult birth. Down in the hole, lingeringly, the grave-digger puts on the forceps.'[13] In Beckett's universe birth is thwarted by the very nature of existence and the imminence of death. In the Whitelaw trilogy the frustration of birth is most clearly ennunciated in *Footfalls*, where May was never born but, in her view, only begun. The voice of the mother indicates this in the second scene of the play:

Where is she, it may be asked. [Pause.] Why in the old home, the same where she—[Pause.] The same where she began. [Pause.] Where it began. [Pause.] It all began. (p. 241)

Beckett himself glossed this passage during the Berlin rehearsals: the mother 'was going to say: ". . . the same where she was *born*". But that is wrong. She just began. "It began. There is a difference. She was never born."'[14]

The central dilemma in *Footfalls*, the dilemma that May exists as an object but has not been born or spiritually animated as a human being, stands at the heart of these three plays. We see the Mouth in *Not I* wrenched by anguish and even erotic power but unable to accept any relation between her physical existence and her mental identity. Thus, the recurring motif: 'what? . . . who? . . . no! . . . she!' The Mouth at her level of denial and suffering persists dramatically into the motion and intensity of May. Of course, this woman has lost the image of her body in the very reduction to mouth, and May first appears in her pacing but then disappears from her story and from our view. These two figures relate as progressive images of that profound dissociation of person that keeps mind and body in tensed opposition.

For May the failure of her own birth is the failure of all women and birth in her world. The mother that we hear in the first two scenes of *Footfalls* becomes in May's narration of scene three, 'Old Mrs. Winter', the figure of sterility. In *Not I* the narrator begins with the rude events of procreation and birth:

parents unknown . . . unheard of . . . he having vanished . . . thin air . . . no sooner buttoned up his breeches . . . she similarly . . . eight months later . . . almost to the tick . . . so no love. (p. 216)

This failure of the sexual and the procreative in *Not I* and *Footfalls* is central to the human deprivation these plays reveal. The collapse of sexual significance and along with it the loss of love are particularly poignant in *Not I*, but the anger against the failure of birth in *Footfalls* is equally powerful.

In *Rockaby*, the images of mother and daughter are superimposed through the rocked woman, the old dress she wears and the rocker itself. In this play Beckett concentrates ideas of life, procreation, nurturing, and death into a single remarkable image. Esslin's idea of a new Beckettian drama based on concretised image applies completely to *Rockaby*. As part of a progression from *Not I* and *Footfalls*, *Rockaby* reveals a further stage in the breakdown between mind and body, between the attempt to comprehend and the impossibility of prevailing against the earth.

In each of these three plays, the intensity of feeling is expressed through a tremendously varied casting of the voice, and through this the sense of aural experience fuses with the visual images of these plays. The *Times* reviewer of the British premiere of *Rockaby* responded to this level of the play when he called *Rockaby* 'a sonata for the actress's voice'.[15] Through a combination of visual and aural images of these female figures Beckett seems to have attained a more direct presentation of emotion and a greater range of expression than through most of his figures of men. In this Whitelaw was probably able to suggest to Beckett both a powerful image of a woman on stage and a range of voice and presence that are rare for any actor. *Not I* is famous for its rapid, nearly hysterical stream of phrases, but *Footfalls* and *Rockaby* also demand the utmost from the actress at the plane of physical vocalization and voice. The slow delivery and low level of speech in *Footfalls* contrast markedly with the tumult of speech in *Not I*, but here the whispers of May are hauntingly tense and dramatic, with concentration and vehemence delivered in a different key than in the earlier play. But the need to remove the self from the world and consciousness along with the sense of the failure of woman and procreation find expression in the two characters of these plays through the resources of the voice.

In *Rockaby* as in *That Time* the thoughts of the character appear to us in the recorded, rhythmic monologue of a voice, but unlike *That Time, Rockaby* requires the presence of the actress's voice, her assertion both of the need for 'more' and her recognition that it is 'time she stopped'. While the addition of the on-stage voice of the woman is subtle, it makes an affirmation of the woman's physicality and her yearning to be released into the inevitability of death. Particularly in the context of *Not I* and *Footfalls, Rockaby* has a vocal theatricality that even Beckett has questioned in the case of *That Time*.

The theme of the frustration of birth and the imagery of the women in these three plays raise a host of questions about Beckett's presentation of women in general. Indeed, it is surprising that so little specifically feminist criticism has been done on Beckett. From the view of the virtues of the feminine within, say, a Jungian approach, Beckett seems to deny the efficacy of symbolic birth or rebirth and to question the concepts of nurturing and emotional fulfilment that might be positively attached to the figures of women. Here, though, Beckett sees his female characters as exposed to the same coldness and unresponsiveness of the cosmos as his male characters. In some ways the problem of birth is particularly charged for the female figure of May, but she shares with Vladimir the sense that spiritual possibility is thwarted by the unconfrontable darkness of existence.

Beckett's focus in this trilogy of plays, *Not I*, *Footfalls*, and *Rockaby*, on the problem of the body and the inefficacy of birth *may* indicate the gender limitations of his writing. This is an issue to be pursued from a feminist perspective. However, Beckett has certainly developed an artistically masterful group of plays through his involvement with the figures of women. Those questions of the interrelations between Molloy, Malone, and the unnameable of the fiction trilogy apply to the women of these plays, and, as in the three novels, so here possibilities of a cyclical progression are intriguing. In fine performance, there can be little doubt that Beckett's concern with the figures of women has led him to the creation of three of his most compelling stage works.

Footfalls, which takes its title from the dominant image of the play, stands as the type of late Beckett drama and the central work of this trilogy based on images of women. Beckett was explicit about the centrality of the pacing of May in his rehearsals for the German premiere of *Footfalls*. As reported by Walter Asmus, '[t]he walking up and down is the central image, he says. This was his basic conception of the play'.[16] As Beckett explicitly claims for the central image in *Footfalls*, so for *Not I* and *Rockaby*, a similar concentration and suggestiveness of a primary visual/dramatic image impresses itself on us during the performance of the play.[17] *Rockaby*, in the continuum with *Not I* and *Footfalls*, likewise presents us with such a dominant image, here of the woman rocking and being rocked—an image that absorbs a remarkable range of associations and levels. And with its companion plays, *Rockaby* has a mesmerizing quality that fuses drama, image, and sound into a strange new spare *Gesamtkunstwerk*. We can see in these three plays Beckett's connection to the late plays of Strindberg, who in turn strove for a visionary and complete kind of drama, that in his case was a distillation of Wagnerian art. Each of these three Beckett plays communicates profoundly through these stage images, each one creates an unforgettable visual, aural, and dramatic effect on the audience, and each of these plays in its own way significantly enlarges our sense of the human.[18]

It may be that Beckett's work in this trilogy, while specifically responding to Whitelaw's abilities as an actress, allowed a projection of this material and himself into the figures of women, a projection that has enlarged the emotional and artistic dimensions of these plays. Along with the meditation on sexuality and the frustration of birth, these plays call our attention to the images of women and the perimeter of the body while at the same time attaining a remarkable dramatic concentration and unity of effect. While Whitelaw found the demands of *Not I* to be unrepeatable after her performance of the play with Beckett, she has recently performed *Footfalls* and *Rockaby* on the same programme, which has helped to reinforce the connection between these works. In these three plays Beckett reaches a rare level, even for him, that combines the paradoxes of existence with spare but haunting imagery and a stunning effect on the 'nerves' of his audience. These dramas of the frustration of birth, language, and self, imply in peripheral vision, the power and the reality of existence, even if the meaning of that existence remains unattainable.

PERSPECTIVE IN *ROCKABY*

JANE ALISON HALE

Samuel Beckett's *Rockaby* premiered in 1981 at the State University of New York at Buffalo, under the direction of Alan Schneider. Beckett's translation of the play into French appeared the following year under the title *Berceuse*.[1]

Rockaby might be characterized as a dramatic poem: Enoch Brater calls it 'a performance poem in the shape of a play'.[2] Its language is not that of everyday life, but rather a condensed and repetitive chant whose rhythm imitates the regular back-and-forth movement of the rocking chair on stage. The French title, *Berceuse*, means both 'rocking chair' and 'lullaby', while the English *Rockaby* refers to a traditional lullaby in which a baby's cradle falls from a tree-top, thus bringing together in one song the images of birth and death which are so often juxtaposed in Beckett. Beckett exploits to the maximum all the illusions, images, and emotions that this old popular musical form can evoke to the eyes, ears, and hearts of his spectators, and the poetry of *Rockaby* closely imitates the soft, repetitive, monotonous, hypnotic lyrics that generations of mothers have sung to lull their infants to sleep. The linguistic and imagistic structure of the play also imitates another form of children's music: the repetitive narrative songs that seem to be coming to an end, only to recommence at the beginning in an endless game of mirrors, e.g. 'Found a Peanut', or 'The Bear Went Over the Mountain'. In one of his rare interviews, Beckett recomended that theatre be made to imitate 'the kind of form one finds in music, . . . where themes keep recurring'.[3] *Rockaby*, which borrows both its title and form from music, is a vivid and successful illustration of this idea. The word 'rockaby' may also call to the minds of some spectators the work 'good-bye', which could also be a fitting title for this dramatic image of a woman approaching her end.

While *Rockaby*'s language suggests the arts of music and of poetry, its visual imagery links it closely with another art: painting. As Billie Whitelaw, Beckett's favourite actress, has so aptly said, 'He writes paintings'.[4] J. D. O'Hara has similarly stated that Beckett's plays 'approach *tableaux vivants*'.[5] And Ruby Cohn has characterised his latest television plays as 'still lives in movement'.[6] Just as the art of painting has undergone a major formal revolution in our century, so has Beckett's drama revolutionized traditional theatrical esthetics. In both domains, the rupture of classical perspective has been a key element of change, and the new perspective of the resulting art works represents the major shift that has taken place in the Western world regarding people's conception of the organization of that world and of their place in it. By perspective, I mean the representation of objects (including other people and the self) in respect to their spatial relationships with one another and with the eye of the observer. *Rockaby* is one of Beckett's latest attempts to define a new dramatic perspective that takes into account the fluctuating, unstable, boundless, impossible nature of vision in a world where human beings no longer occupy the privileged, exterior, and omniscient point of view of the classical artist.

The 'story' told by the words of *Rockaby* is quite simple, condensing into several oft-repeated formulas the essentials of an entire human existence:

the day came
when she said
time she stopped
going to and fro
all eyes
for another
another creature like herself
went back in
time she went and sat
at her window
facing other windows
all eyes
for another
all blinds down
hers alone up
when she said
time she stopped
went down
down the steep stair
into the old rocker
where mother sat
all in black
sat and rocked
with closed eyes
saying to the rocker
rock her off

Thus, as we learn from the voice to which we are listening, the woman we see upon the stage has spent her life in pursuit of vision, desperately searching to see—another like herself, or herself—and to be seen. She finally renounces this effort and disappears before our eyes, an indication that human existence is nothing more nor less than a continual, albeit fruitless, struggle for perception. Vision, its conditions and its impossibility, are therefore the central concern of *Rockaby*, as well as of much of Beckett's oeuvre.

The text of *Rockaby* comprises four parts, the first three of which are roughly equal in length (52, 57, and 58 lines respectively), while the fourth is half as long again as the preceding sections (84 lines). Each successive part contains a limited number of different lines, some of which echo words, lines, and passages from previous sections, with or without variations, and some of which are new, but may be repeated in the following section(s). Beckett's fascination with the process of permutation is evident in his skilful manipulation of *Rockaby*'s restricted number of words, sounds, and images.

The sole image of *Rockaby* is that of a woman, prematurely old and dressed in black, who sits in a rocking chair listening to her own recorded voice. Each part of the play begins in precisely the same manner: the immobility of the rocker, the woman's voice asking for 'More', another pause, and the simultaneous commencement of the rock (which is controlled mechanically) and the recorded voice, whose first two lines are similar throughout and identical in parts one and three ('till in the end/the day came') and in parts two and four ('so in the end/close of a long day'). Each section ends with the simultaneous echo of the last line, the coming to rest of the rock, and a faint fade of light (which becomes a slow total fade-out at the end). The last two verses of each part are either identical ('rock her off/rock her off'—part four) or nearly so ('another living soul/one other living soul'—part two), and parts one and three again repeat each other ('time she stopped/*time she stopped*', with the italicized line being spoken by both the woman on stage and her recorded voice). Such meticulous construction and repetitiveness are not confined to the beginnings and endings of each part of *Rockaby*, but are evident throughout the play.

We must remember that the woman we see is listening to her own voice, which is coming to her from outside, as did Krapp in *Krapp's Last Tape* and the old face of *That Time*. This now-familiar Beckettian technique serves both to indicate to the spectators that we are penetrating the consciousness of the mute character on stage and to dramatise the dual nature of human perception—the division of every consciousness into a perceiving subject and a perceived object that can never coincide with each other, in spite of all one's desires to join them in a perfect perception of the self.

The lighting, consisting of a subdued light on the rocker that becomes slightly weaker at the end of each part, and a constant spot on the woman's face, suggests the light of human consciousness as it endeavours constantly, yet unsuccessfully, to perceive itself up till the very moment of its extinction. The subdued, concentrated, and fading light, the woman's black costume, her grey hair, her white hands and face, produce the visual impression of a life and a world that are in the process of disappearing. Black and white, the predominant colours of Beckett's latest works, evoke for him the undifferentiation of the void, towards which tend human life and all the perceptual efforts of which it consists from the very moment of birth. At the end of the play, the light, the voice, and the movement of the rocker fade away simultaneously with our visual and auditory perception of this diminishing human existence.

Having given up her travels in the outer world where she had searched, all eyes, all sides, high and low, for another like herself, the woman has come back inside. At first she sits quietly at her window, waiting for the appearance of her other at a neighbouring window, but she finally renounces even this hope and descends the steep stair of her consciousness where she meets, not herself, but the image of her mother who had spent her life seeking the same impossible goals. The narration of all these voyages, both exterior and interior, follows the slight, slow, regular rhythm of the rocking chair, a privileged image for Beckett ever since the novel *Murphy*, where the character sought refuge in his rocking chair in order to live and see clearly in his mind. Since the time of *Murphy*, Beckett seems to have lost faith in the possibility of freeing the mind from all influences of the external world, but he has retained his predilection for the controlled, rhythmic movement of the rocker. For Beckett, movement is the fundamental characteristic of all that exists in time and space, and it is the veil which hinders our vision of both the external world and our interior selves.[7] All of his characters wander through time and space in pursuit of another living soul or of themselves. From the voyages in geographical space of his early novels to the internal explorations of the consciousness undertaken by the characters of his latest plays, the difficulty remains the same: the inexorable flux, change, and movement which preclude the attainment of a fixed, stable point that would finally permit vision. Realising that it is impossible to become immobile in time and space, the Beckettian character nevertheless prefers to bring the ineluctable movement of life under control by making it as continous and steady as possible. If all movement is without goal or direction, if every step forward is negated by a step backward, if all hope of meeting the longed-for other is merely an illusion, then wisdom consists of accepting this situation and giving oneself over to the comforting sway of the old rocker which goes continuously back and forth with no other goal than to control and give form to the movement that cannot be escaped so long as one is alive.

Here then is what we, the spectators of *Rockaby*, see with our eyes as we look at the stage: a woman sitting in a rocker listening to herself. But we 'see' something else in our minds, a vision at one remove, as we listen to this woman's words describe the endless struggle for vision that has characterised her life. Let us examine her words closely in order to discover what she sees, what she has attempted unsuccessfully to see during her life, and the way in which she, and Beckett, communicate these perceptions to the spectators. The fourth part of the text will be used to structure this analysis, since most of the lines and images of the previous parts are repeated in this final section, but reference will be made to the other sections when appropriate.

The voice begins its fourth set of lines with the same words it spoke at the beginning of part two: 'so in the end/close of a long day'. But here it is referring to *another* long day: at the end of the day in part two, the woman had come back in from her wanderings in the outside world where she had gone to and fro in search of another like herself. This time, however, she abandons her wait at the window, where she had at first been looking for her other, sitting at a window facing hers, and then, simply another blind up, like hers, 'one blind up no more'. Renouncing her hope ever to be able to see or be seen by *another* living soul in the external world, she has let down her blind and descended the steep stair to sit in the old rocker where her mother had once sat, and where we now, perhaps, see her upon the stage. The word 'down' is repeated six times in the first seven lines of this final section, while it is used only once in the preceding sections ('all blinds down'). This repetition of 'down', coupled with the play's first mention of the 'steep stair', gives verbal shape and force to the internal descent that is about to be recounted. The woman is descending into the depths of her self, embarking upon an internal voyage in pursuit of that inaccessible essence where the perceiving 'I' and the perceived 'me' would coincide, where the desire for perception would be fulfilled, where the ceaseless, obsessive, and futile wandering that characterizes human existence might finally reach its goal.

The language of the text suggests the labyrinthine character of these inner depths. No image or situation evoked brings the description to even a momentary resting place, but each leads imperceptibly into another. The word 'down', for instance, ties together a series of actions that are presented nonchronologically: the woman's descent of the stairs, her letting down of the blind, and her sinking into the rocking chair. The fourth line, 'in the end went down', combines words from both lines one—'so in the end'—and three—'went down', just as the entire fourth section, from its very beginning, repeats many words and lines heard previously in the play. The nonchronological, repetitious, spiraling, cumulative, fluid language of *Rockaby* corresponds to the nature of the consciousness it is intended to portray.

When the voice says 'into the old rocker', referring for the first time to the rocking chair we have been looking at since the beginning of the play, we have the momentary impression that the words to which we are listening have finally caught up with the image before our eyes. However, this encounter is fleeting and uncertain, because the text immediately resumes its distance from the stage image as it draws us into a verbal and imagistic game of mirrors, using the word 'rocker' to link images of present and past: the 'old rocker' where the woman sits becomes first a 'mother rocker', then the rocker 'where mother sat', 'sat and rocked', 'all the years/all in black/best black', 'till her end came', just as her daughter, at whom we are looking, and who is also dressed 'all in black/best black', will rock on till the end of the play. The end of the mother, alluded to in the lines 'till her end came/in the end came', echoes the end of the long day mentioned in the first lines of this section, where the voice was describing the end of a day in the daughter's life. We have thus gone back in time, from the close of one day in the past of the woman on stage, to rejoin the image of her mother, 'gone off her head', who had sat and rocked, and have journeyed forward from that time to the moment of the mother's death, which occurred one night: 'dead one night/in the rocker/in her best black/head fallen/and the rocker rocking/rocking away'. We may also be anticipating here yet another time, a future point in the life of the woman on stage, which we shall witness at the play's conclusion as her 'Head slowly sinks, comes to rest' before the final fade-out. The boundaries between mother and daughter become less and less defined as the text moves back and forth in time, from one black-clad woman in a rocker to another, using similar or identical words, phrases, and rhythms to tie together a series of non-identical, yet somehow indistinguishable, images.

Here we are, thus, in the middle of part four, at our starting point: 'in the end/close of a long day'. But which one? The close of the day when 'her' mother died? Or the 'close of a long day' of the beginning of the play? Or the one which begins part two? Or part three? Or part four? Or perhaps the one we witness at the conclusion of the play? All we can know for certain is that we are moving in time, accompanied by the rhythmic, repetitive words of the voice and the concrete image of the slowly-moving rocker which lull our minds just as they do the woman on stage. In other words, the reconstruction of this woman's life in linear perspective is impossible for the spectator, whom she draws into the depths of her consciousness. The lack of traditional syntax and punctuation in the text, as well as the dull, expressionless voice of the actress[8] contributes to this destruction of geometric perspective: we never know exactly at which point one image or memory ends and another begins.

Ruby Cohn contrasts the temporality of Beckett's drama with that of classical theatre as follows: 'whereas classical peripetias thrill through to a conclusion, Beckett's plays are unfinal. Rather than Aristotelian beginning, middle, and end, Beckett's plays are endless continua.'[9] To the endless continuum of *Rockaby*, Beckett joins a boundless theatrical space that Cohn has labelled 'theatereality':

> In the pre-*Play* (1962) plays Beckett gains tension between a strange setting and verbal glimpses of other places; in the post-*Play* plays fictional and theater situation and place can converge—theatereality.
>
> . . .
>
> In Beckett's theater plays of the 1970s (and 1980s), containing theatereality, tension grows between the spare invariant settings and the memories of lived-in places.[10]

So we find ourselves, with the woman at whom we are looking, at the end of one long day or another, in an indeterminate space that is nevertheless presented to our eyes—it little matters which day or which place, since they are all basically so alike. A woman—mother? daughter? or another?—dressed in her best black, just like the character on stage, rocks away in her rocker, and the text repeats exactly the first eight lines of the beginning of part four: 'so in the end/close of a long day/went down/in the end went down/down the steep stair/let down the blind and down/right down/into the old rocker'. This time, instead of calling the rocker 'mother rocker', the voice alludes to the rocker's maternal embrace with the words, 'those arms at last'. This woman has spent her entire life trying to see and be seen by another. Having finally admitted the impossibility of her quest, she consoles herself as best she can in the embrace of the old 'mother rocker'. She is far from the first Beckettian character to seek the maternal embrace at the end of her life, to attempt to return to her mother's womb where she would be rocked to her final sleep, just as her own mother had met her end in the arms of the very same rocker.

Beckett's notes to *Rockaby* indicate that the woman on stage, whose eyes are 'now closed, now open in unblinking gaze', and increasingly closed as the play advances, are to close definitively 'halfway through [section] 4', presumably at the lines: 'with closed eyes/closing eyes'. The words of the text thus correspond once again, momentarily, to the image we see, but they re-establish their distance immediately as they resume telling the story of this woman, or another, who had searched high and low, to see, to be seen. The word 'eyes' is used to unify the various temporal levels of the text at this point, as it appears in four successive lines: 'with closed eyes/closing eyes/she so long all eyes/famished eyes'. The closed eyes, which might be thought to indicate a conclusion to the compulsive persuit of vision of which this woman's life has consisted, do not afford her consciousness even a momentary respite from the process of perception. While the eyes on stage remain closed, the woman's inner vision is related to us by her recorded voice, as the closed eyes move backwards in time to become 'closing eyes', and then the wide-open eyes of a person famished for an impossible vision, the eyes of the woman who cannot escape her need 'to see/be seen' even when she closes her eyes in the dark sanctuary of her mother rocker. She will acknowledge this inevitability of perception in the play's final lines, when, with her eyes closed, her voice begs the rocker to 'stop her eyes/rock her off'.

The blind which the woman had let down over her window, and which is mentioned both before and after the closing of the eyes, corresponds to the lids she has just closed over her eyes, those 'posterns of the mind',[11] which had for so long gazed out upon a world where there was nothing to see, just as the window of her house had never offered any nourishment to her famished eyes. However, neither the lowering of the blind nor that of the eyelids has stemmed her desire to perceive.

After hearing the voice's final recollection of the woman's fruitless travels 'high and low/to and fro', and then of her vigil 'at her window', in hopes of seeing or being seen by another, we are told once more of her decision to stop seeking her other at her window. This decision was first announced in part three by the lines, 'till the day came/in the end came/close of a long day', reiterated at the opening of part four, beginning with the words, 'so in the end/close of a long day', again in the middle of this part with the same introduction, 'so in the end/close of a long day', and here prefaced by similar lines, 'till in the end/close of a long day'.

As the woman leaves the window, she says 'to herself/whom else/time she stopped'. It is time she stopped looking for another in the outside world, since there is nobody to see, or even talk to, but herself. She wishes therefore to be henceforth 'her own other', the 'other living soul' she has always sought, but she will not succeed in seeing herself, either. The repetition of the familiar refrain, 'so in the end/close of a long day', just before the final lines that deal with the woman's efforts to be 'her own other', suggests that this last attempt at perception will repeat the failure of all the previous ones.

Several times during the play the voice (usually joined by the voice of the woman on stage) has told us that the woman said to herself, 'time she stopped', but now the line 'saying to herself' is corrected by a 'no/done with that', and the voice tells the rocker to 'rock her off'. This phrase calls to mind the expression 'off her rocker', which further links the woman in question to her mother, who had 'gone off her head'. By asking the rocking chair to 'rock her off', the woman expresses her desire to give up talking to herself because the creature she has been seeking, first in the external world, eyes open, then inside herself, eyes closed, can never be reached either by her eyes or by her words. The internal self is as multiple, fugitive, and nonexistent as are the other living souls she had sought from her window before her descent down the steep stair of her consciousness. We become lost in the text to the extent that we no longer know whether 'she' refers to the woman on stage, another, her mother, or even the rocking chair (especially in the French version, where 'la berceuse' is referred to as 'elle'), because Beckett has succeeded in making us reproduce the unfocused and fleeting vision of a consciousness that meets the object of its desire only temporarily and in a fragmented form, losing sight of it at the very instant when that consciousness, and we the spectators, believe we have finally achieved our goal of vision.

What Ruby Cohn has written of Beckett's earlier play *Not I* applies equally well to the effect produced by *Rockaby* upon its spectators:

> We see and hear through the voice-brain conflict. Our minds 'pick it up,' seeking sense through the segmented syntax, staccato rhythms, and few swiftly sketched events. Beckett has conceived a whole play as soliloquy, in which he withholds knowledge of its protagonist only to immerse us all the more deeply in an emotional relationship with her.[12]

The woman of *Rockaby* must now be content to feel the arms of the rocking chair and to speak to it, in the third person, of herself and of her aborted existence which has consisted merely of one long effort to see and be seen, to see another or herself, to be seen by another or by herself. This hope, which proved to be so futile, has nevertheless motivated the entire life which she has just described to us and which we have seen pass before our eyes and in our imaginations in the form of fluctuating and inextricably interwoven characters, moments, images, and words. Beckett once wrote about the painting of the Van Velde brothers, which he admired so greatly, in words that apply equally well to the esthetics of *Rockaby*: 'un dévoilement sans fin, voile derrière voile, plan sur plan de transparences imparfaites, un dévoilement vers l'indévoilable, le rien, la chose à nouveau.'[13]

The line, 'stop her eyes', which is repeated twice near the end of the text, was omitted in the French translation. Such an omission is characteristic of Beckett's translations, which are often less explicit and more ambigious than the original texts. The voice's order to 'stop her eyes' indicates that, in order for the woman to be able to 'stop', a desire she has often expressed since the beginning of the play, her eyes must first cease to function. For life is nothing more nor less than the act of perception or the state of being perceived, or, in the words of Bishop Berkeley which find echoes throughout Beckett's work, 'esse est percipi'.[14]

The final ten lines of text are the least repetitive of the entire play. Although they contain many familiar words and sounds, only one of these lines has been heard before ('those arms at last'). The novelty of the last lines is all the more striking because they follow a group of eleven lines that echo previous passages of *Rockaby*. The newest, and most shocking, of the concluding lines is 'fuck life'; its effect is extremely strong not only because of the obscenity it contains, but also because neither word in it has yet been spoken during the play. The corresponding French line, 'aux gogues la vie', has a similar shock effect, although its meaning is somewhat different. 'Gogues' is a little-used vulgar word for 'chamber pot', and Beckett's choice of it is proof that, in translating, he pays at least as much attention to the sound of words as to their meaning.

At the end of the play we perceive the nearly simultaneous cessation of the voice, the rocking, and the image of the woman in the rocker. It almost seems that her prayers have been answered, that her relentless pursuit of self, and the third-person commentary she has been offering upon it, have finally come to an end, with her life and with her consciousness, which are extinguished at the same moment as the stage lights. However, at the last moment of the play, when everything comes to a standstill, the lighting does not go out all at once: we see it fade first upon the chair and, after a 'long pause with spot on face alone', when the 'head slowly sinks, comes to rest', the final light fades slowly out and the woman's face disappears into the void. The brief interval between the extinction of the two stage lights of *Rockaby* calls to mind a similar use of lighting at the end of *A Piece of Monologue*. In both cases, Beckett is dramatising a problem which has long intrigued him: the temporal gap that must occur at the moment of death between the perceiving consciousness and its object, the perceived self. For, at the very moment when the object of perception, the woman, finally becomes immobile in time and space, i.e. a fixed and therefore visible object, she ceases to exist, she is no longer herself. Her consciousness thus goes out without even fulfilling its goal, since it can succeed in being its own 'other' neither in life nor in death. However, the image of this woman and of her consciousness, which we have just penetrated, will remain for quite a while before our eyes and in our minds, just as those of her mother had not been completely extinguished at the close of that long day when she died, but continue to be present to the perception of her daughter, and thus to ours. And they may well reappear to this daughter's daughter when she closes her eyes and rocks till her end in the arms of her mother rocker one night, at the close of a long day. And perhaps also to *this* daughter's daughter, who will set the entire process in motion once again when she asks the voice to tell her about her own life, which is so like that of her mother and her mother's mother, and so like that which we all live. It is a life which, just like this play which begins with the command 'More', has neither beginning nor end, and is simply a search to see and be seen, but where vision occurs only in bits, pieces, and obscure reflections in an infinite game of mirrors.

KNOW HAPPINESS: IRONY IN *ILL SEEN ILL SAID*

MONIQUE NAGEM

Samuel Beckett's publication *Ill Seen Ill Said* is a complex, ironic narrative whose textual features reflect a strategy meant to excoriate the labour of the writer. As a result, in the words of Wallace Stevens, '. . . We cannot tell apart/ The idea and the bearer-being of the idea. / . . . The poem is the cry of its occasion,/ Part of the res itself and not about it.'[1]

The first problem which *Ill Seen Ill Said* presents is a generic one. In its first publication in English it appeared in the *New Yorker* in 1981 as a short story or novella. However, as Marjorie Perloff states in a recent article, such a classification of the text is erroneous.[2] By scanning its first few lines, she demonstrates that they bear more resemblance to verse than to prose. The opening paragraph of *ISIS* reads as follows:

> From where she lies she sees Venus rise. On. From where she lies when the skies are clear she sees Venus rise followed by the sun. Then she rails at the source of all life. On. At evening when the skies are clear she savours its star's revenge.[3]

Perloff rearranges the lines of this opening paragraph and scans them thus:

From whére she líes
she sees Vénus ríse.
Ón.
From whére she líes
when the skíes are cléar
she seés Vénus ríse
fóllowed by the sún
Then she ráils at the sóurce of âll lífe.
Ón.
At évening when the skíes are cléar
she sávours its stár's revénge.[4]

She concludes that this passage, which could be called a strophe, is made up of 'Six dimeter lines, five of them rhyming, followed by three trimeters made up primarily of anapests, the whole bound together by the alliteration of voices and voiceless spirants [. . .] and punctuated twice by the refrain word "On"'.[5] Yet the text cannot be called verse because Beckett did not choose to lineate it. In addition not all passages resemble poetry as this one does. Others simulate prose. Perloff calls this prose-verse ambiguity 'free prose'.[6] The erasure of the boundaries between prose and verse began in the nineteenth century as exemplified by the lyrical attainments of Flaubert's *Salammbô* and Mallarmé's descriptive poems. Baudelaire had led the way in this creative enterprise, which has been even more fully explored by modern writers.[7] However genre fusion is only one of the late nineteenth century poets' creative innovations which modern writers, including Beckett, have inherited and reworked. The late nineteenth century was also the time for that momentous rebellion against empiricism and its impact on literature. According to poets like Baudelaire, Nerval, Rimbaud, and Mallarmé, the literary text is not a transparent replication of the 'world/reality' whose language reveals a static meaning amenable to interpretation, but rather an ambiguous, polysemous unity which functions as a vehicle for exploring an undisclosed world, for searching for a quasi-mystical centre of consciousness and its relations with some transcendental principle.[8] With Mallarmé also begins the poem which questions itself about the essence of poetising. Octavio Paz states that Mallarmé invented the 'critical poem', which is not a recipe book in the fashion of traditional versified 'poetic arts' but an inquiry into the peculiar truth of the poem.[9] Twentieth century poets and novelists continued the revolution, poets such as Yeats, Pound, and Eliot; novelists such as Woolf, Joyce, and Proust. The movement led to further experimentation as exemplified by Surrealist texts and the 'nouveau roman', for instance. The different manifestations which announced the erosion of a positivist epistemology and the creation of a new one include, in addition to the experimentations of the nineteenth century *Symbolistes*, a growing lack of confidence, on the part of writers in a logical order of human rationality resulting in the production of fragmented, non-linear, and sometimes achronic texts. Samuel Beckett, whose literary career spans the pre-World War II years to the present, has written novels some critics have classified as modernist, others as 'nouveau roman', and yet others as post-modernist, and plays which have inaugurated the Theatre of the Absurd; Beckett's poetry however has received very little critical attention.[10] *ISIS*, published approximately a century after Mallarmé's *Crise de vers*, constitutes an elaboration of the experimentations of the *Symbolistes* and their descendants, written in the ironic mode.

In *Anatomy of Criticism* Northrop Frye classifies fictions into five different modes: myth, romance, tragedy, comedy, and irony. In the mode of irony he classifies the French *Symbolistes* who 'begin with the ironic gesture of turning away from the world of the market-place, with all its blurred sounds and imprecise meanings: they renounce rhetoric, moral judgement, and all other idols of the tribe, and devote their entire energy to the poet's literal function as a maker of poems'.[11] In *ISIS* Beckett transforms the conventions of the symbolist canon, to which poets are diverse as Paul Valéry, St. John Perse, Wallace Stevens and Hart Crane can be said to belong. The structuring strategy of *ISIS* is the embedding of two 'stories', that of an old woman who resides in an isolated cabin amidst sepulchral stones, and that of the artist creating the old woman's story, or more exactly, in this case, recording her movements and her surroundings. The first text is closed, cyclical, and atemporal; the second is open, linear, and temporal. The former is the rendering of symbolist conventions in an ironic mode, the second is a transgression of the conventions of the 'critical poem'.

According to Sharon Spencer, a novel with a closed structure 'embodies a single exclusively maintained perspective, [. . .] is a self-sustaining creation, free from outside influences (except for the perspective of the reader), from the "laws" of logic and causality, and from what is usually called "credibility": [. . .] a unique original world, complete in itself'.[12] The story of the old woman in *ISIS* is a self-sustaining creation free from the laws of logic. The woman is seen from the single perspective of the eye observing her, her world defies the laws of credibility: she lives in total isolation in a barren cabin surrounded by twelve mysterious guardians, in an atmosphere of mystery, death, and desolation. There is no world outside the woman's preoccupation with a single stone she visits regularly, or her intense desire to see the star Venus rise. Causality is also non-existent. The reader ignores why the old woman is where she is or why she is doing what she is doing. Temporality exists only in the mentions of the season: it is always winter, and the time of day: it is always dawn or evening/night. The period setting is unknown; not even the woman's clothes provide a clue. The duration of events is vague. At one point there is a mention of the woman's having been absent for several months; otherwise no other reference of duration is made. Certain narrative and rhetorical features of this text not only reflect its self-containment and its atemporality but also become functional parts of its strategy: circularity. A microcosm of that strategy is evident in the sentence, 'Black as jade the jasper that flecks its whiteness'. (p. 44) In view of the fact that the only colours which govern the text are black and white (with the exception of the woman's 'washen blue eye') the sentence seems a paradoxical way of describing the rough-hewn granite of the stone to which the woman is drawn. Jade is a mineral whose colour ranges from white to green. How then can black qualify it? Furthermore, jasper is an opaque variety of quartz which is reddish brown or yellow in colour. However, the phrase can be returned to the bi-chromatic tones of the whole text, if another definition for the word jade is applied; jade can also mean a worthless woman or a broken down old nag. The word, in that case, would match the description of the old woman who, dressed all in black, whose hair is white, duplicates the black and white pattern. In addition, when the word jasper is accompanied by the noun, ware, it refers to a fine white porcelain, often coloured by metallic oxides with raised designs remaining white. Just as the sentence returns on itself like the magical ourobouros, the text recounting the old woman's story becomes a compendium of circles and cycles.

The most evident dispersion of circles occurs on the verbal level. Each chapter or strophe, contains an obvious preponderance of words containing the letter 'o'. It can be the repetition of a word like 'on', or it can be the proliferation of words containing a double 'o' like gloom, doomed, moon, moor, aloof, door, grooved, cooped, roof, floor, wooed, sooner, droops, spoon, brood, too soon, balloon, (the latter having a round signified); many of these words are repeated within one paragraph as in strophe 13 the word buttonhook is used once, hook twice, and hooking once, supported by another of their kind 'boots'(p. 18). Another evidence of the circle on the verbal level is the large number of sentences lavish in an unusually high number of words containing the letter 'o'. A few of the more obvious ones will serve as examples:

The eye glued to one or the other window. (p. 12)

[. . .] not for long. For slowly it emerges again. Rises from the floor and slowly up to lose itself in the gloom. The semi-gloom. (p. 22)

Under the low lowering sky the north is lost. Obliterated by the snow [. . .] (p. 33)

[. . .] wholly gone. Why none but to open no more. Till all done She done. Or left undone. (p. 37-38)

No loss of pallor. None of cold. (p. 48)

Prominent among those sentences is the phrase 'zone of stones' which refers to an area within the boundaries of the old woman's world. Among those stones is one in particular which she visits regularly. In this case, not only is there the repetition of the 'o' but also the lugubrious and cavernous sounds of zone and stone which echo the area's true function which is that of a cemetery. On the rhetorical level the circle dominates also. The woman's territorial limits are circumscribed by a circle, 'The two zones form a roughly circular whole. As though outlined by a trembling hand' (p. 9). In addition there are many references to round objects, such as the black hat which the woman owns, the eye which constantly observes her, and a dial described as a white disc.

Closely associated with the circle is the cycle which Beckett emphasizes with the numerous descriptions of the woman standing at her window waiting for Venus to appear in the sky, followed by the sun, then again waiting for its reappearance at night. In addition, the temporal references are usually to dawn and to night, in cycles. The cycles of the stars and of the days are reinforced by the cycle of the cardinal points which encircle the woman and her cabin:

> The sun that once beat down. So east and west sides the required clash. (p. 43)
>
> When from their source in the west-south-west the last rays rake its averse face. (p. 44)
>
> Lit aslant by the latest last rays they cast to the east-north-east their long parallel shadows. (p. 44)
>
> Sends her wavering north and south from wall to wall. (p. 47)

The cycle can even be detected in the etymology of words such as 'embers' which means remains of a dying fire, but when it is capitalised refers to the religious Ember days, the recurring days of fasting during each season of the year. The word comes from the Old English *ymbrendagas* which comes from *ymbryne* which means a 'running around' or a circuit.

What does this proliferation of circles mean? The circle symbolises infinity as well as void, as the narrator of *ISIS* intimates, 'As to zero the infinite' (p. 54). For Plato the circle was the symbol of perfection, for Parmenides, of being; in the Middle Ages it symbolised God, in the Renaissance, the universe, and for Pascal, existential despair. Circularity is a topos in many of Beckett's works; it is evident for instance in his play *Waiting for Godot* where two acts repeat the same action; it is also manifest in his novel *Molloy* where the quests of both Molloy and Moran lead back to the beginning of the text. In using the circle as a generative device, Beckett not only acknowledges the multiplicity of the circle's symbolic references, he also foregrounds the *symbolistes*' symbol of the Absolute. This search for an absolute, for a transcendental principle which consumed the *symbolistes* and in particular Mallarmé, is here parodied on the thematic level in the 'story' of the old woman. Mallarmé's descent into the *Néant* (void) and his ceaseless search for an absolute, Beauty, is reenacted in many of his poems. In an unpublished essay on *ISIS* Marjorie Perloff has uncovered a multitude of parodic allusions to what she describes as 'En. Lit. canon'. For example a line such as 'Closed again to that end the vile jelly or opened again of left as it was however that was' (p. 52), is an allusion to Shakespeare's *King Lear*: 'Out vile jelly. Where is thy lustre now?'[13] She also finds the language of *ISIS* cast in a Pre-Raphaelite or Yellow nineties style similar to that of Dowson, Symons, Wilde, and the early Yeats. It is probable that more examples of such intertextuality could be added to the already numerous ones Perloff has found, including a possible archetype for the old woman in Pater's line, 'older than the rocks among which she sits'. However in her comparison between the French and the English version of *ISIS*, Perloff contests that the French version *Mal vu mal dit*, presumably written first, then translated into English by its author, is free of such linguistic, metrical, and semantic allusions. In fact she concludes that that was Beckett's initial reason for choosing to write in French rather than in English, to free his language of his ancestral literary tradition. Yet, there is another feature of *ISIS* which Perloff did not examine and that is its allusions to the *symbolistes*, primarily to Mallarmé (another name beginning with the letter 'm') and to the conventions of post-symbolist poets. Certain elements in the woman's 'story' considered in isolation might simply be inconsequential allusions to Mallarmé, but in view of their numbers and in combination with the structure and the theme of the 'story', they become signs of Beckett's less than innocent transgressions. For instance the beginning of one paragraph, 'Incontinent the void. The zenith.' includes the downward and the upward movement of many of Mallarmé's poems: the poet's descent into the void before he can reach toward the Absolute. In addition, the 'zenith' echoes Mallarmé's famous 'azur'. The word void is repeated numerous times throughout *ISIS*. The following alliterations are worthy of Mallarmé, had he composed in English, 'must murmur. Moonless star-studded sky' (p. 42). When the eye observing the old woman concentrates on objects such as the buttonhook which hangs on the wall, the key the old woman holds, the grass around her, or her hair, they shimmer, or tremble, or shiver; the eye observes an 'infinitesimal quaver', an 'imperceptible tremor'. In Mallarmé's *Crise de vers* a precedent for this vibration was established:

A quoi bon la merveille de transférer un fait de nature en sa presque disparition vibratoire selon le jeu de la parole, cependant; si ce n'est pour qu'en émane, sans la gène d'un proche ou contret rappel, la notion pure.[14]

In a 1868 letter to his friend Cazallis, Mallarmé wrote a description for the proposed setting of his sonnet 'Ses purs ongles', which uncannily resembles the old woman's cabin setting in *ISIS*

Par exemple, une fenêtre nocturne ouverte, les deux volets attachés; une chambre avec personne dedans, malgré l'air stable que représentent les volets attachés, et dans une nuit faite d'absence et d'interrogation, sans meubles, sinon l'ébauche plausible de vagues consoles, un cadre belliqueux et agonisant, de miroir appendu au fond, avec sa reflexion, stellaire et incomprehensible, de la grande Ourse qui relie au ciel seul ce logis abandonné au monde.[15]

The old woman's cabin is also abandoned to the world, almost empty, surrounded by night. As Mallarmé's room is linked to the sky by the Big Bear Constellation, so the cabin of the old woman is by the star Venus. *ISIS* also bears an uncanny resemblance to another of Mallarmé's texts of undetermined genre, 'Igitur'. As in *ISIS*, a voice or consciousness closely watches and records the every move of a person. The mysterious twelve guardians which surround the old woman are also prefigured in 'Igitur' which ends with the following cryptic stage direction: '"Ne sifflez pas" aux vents, aux ombres—si je compte, comédien, jouer le tour—les 12—pas de hasard sans aucun sens.'[16] Such more or less explicit allusions to the master *symboliste*, Mallarmé, as well as to his English counterparts, are what Gérard Genette calls *relations transtextuelles* which include everything which places in manifest or secret relation one text with other texts.[17] In the case of *ISIS* and the *Symbolistes*, relations are secret, that is one can only point to the similarities, the echoes which link *ISIS* to 'Igitur' for example in such an uncanny fashion. However when the links are examined in combination with the mystical and mythical thematics of the old woman's 'story', certain assumptions can be made about Beckett's strategy. It is possible that the old woman is an avatar of Hérodiade, the young blond beauty of Mallarmé's poem of the same name, as well as Salomé and the other *femmes fatales* of the late nineteenth century. Only now she is old and a widow, 'And the old body itself. [. . .] Beneath the weeds' mock calm' (p. 30). If the word weeds denotes the widow's weeds, then the old woman's numerous trips to a stone among many others which resemble tombstones are probably visits to her husband's grave. Her hair is now white. The objects around her, like the buttonhook, the key, the steps, are worn. Her life has become static and sterile. When her hands are being scrutinised by the eye, they rest 'On its sole pubis. Dead still to be sure' (p. 32). The star she intensely desires to see, named for Venus, the goddess of love and femininity only reminds her of her sterility, 'Mindful perhaps of evenings when she was able too late' (p. 47). Her surroundings are as sterile as she. Her only neighbours are sepulchres, the time of day is always evening or night, the season is always winter and snow covers her world. Hérodiade has become Hecate, the goddess of the moon, of the night, of the underworld. The mythological Hecate was often associated with the crocus, the only flowers which bloom in the old woman's world; one of her symbols was the key, which the old woman carries with her, and her sacred animal was the lamb, an animal which also is part of the old woman's environment. The chalky soil which invades the grass is said to resemble lambs; the fifth strophe is replete with references to lambs, 'White splotches in the grass. Aloof from the unheeding ewes' (p. 11). Apparently they too are sterile. At one time the old woman is described walking followed by a lamb. As goddess of the moon, Hecate fits the circular motif which recurs in the text: the moon resembles a zero, which is both nothing, and the infinite. Twelve is also a number which shares in the perfection of the circle and the cycle, and which connotes mythical allusions. The guardians who surround the old woman are numbered twelve, a mystical number associated with Christ, the twelve apostles, New Jerusalem. It is also the number of the signs of the zodiac, of the winds, and the lunar months. These twelve are what keep the old woman in the centre so that she is caught inside a mystical ring within which she travels, 'To cross it in a straight line takes her from five to ten minutes' (p. 8). 'Diameter. [. . .] Say one furlong. On an average. Beyond the unknown' (p. 9). Symbolist poets, sensitive to the universal vastness which reaches us in fragmented form, posit the poem as a liminal space between the phenomenal and the noumenal worlds. In Beckett's text the transcendental principle is more problematic. If a *Symboliste*, like Mallarmé, viewed the mystical experience as a downward movement into the *Néant* followed by an upward movement toward the Absolute, Beckett views the movement arrested in its downward position. The old woman/Hecate belongs to the demonic imagery rather than the apocalypic. Northrop Frye defines the apocalyptic symbolism as presenting 'The infinitely desirable, in which the lusts and ambitions of man are identified with, adapted to, or projected on the gods'.[18] It is an art of 'innocence'. The demonic pattern is related to the analogy of experience, and its metaphorical identities include evening and night, sea or snow, age and death, autumn and winter.[19] The old woman's world is all these in addition to feeling 'at times of being below sea level'.(p. 9) Her world is static, the circle or the cycle does not go anywhere, her movements are repetitious and amount to no more than following the diameter within the circular surface delimited by the twelve. Like the swan in Mallarmé's sonnet 'Le vierge, le vivace et le bel aujourd'hui', she is trapped in eternal exile. Space and time have merged as the eye's description of the mysterious dial introduced in a close up demonstrates:

White disc divided in minutes. Unless it be in seconds. Sixty black dots. No figure. One hand only. Finest of fine black darts. It advances by fits and starts. No tick. Leaps from dot to dot with so lightning a leap that but for its new position it had not stirred. [. . .] Having thus covered after its fashion assuming the instrument plumb the first quarter of its latest hour. Unless it be its latest minute. Then doubt certain—then despair certain nights of its ever attaining the last. Ever regaining north. (pp. 45-46)

The disc is at once a watch dial and a compass; at once time and space.

Beckett's treatment of the old woman's 'story' in the ironic mode also reveals itself in the text's linguistic prowess. In the first place the text is replete with oxymorons, a rhetorical antithesis which etymologically means 'pointedly foolish'. A few examples will illustrate: the tomb which is a silent world, as it spreads, is said to be responsible for a din. (p. 28)

She on the contrary immaculately black. (p. 33)
Imaginary murmur of flakes beating on the roof. (p. 34)
Incontinent the void. (p. 39)
[. . .] the limp grass strangely rigid. (p. 42)
[. . .] recent future. (p. 57)

There are several scatological references. For example the phrase 'incontinent the void' appears to be a tautology; the first word can mean not being able to control excretory functions, and void means to evacuate body wastes; one seems to refer to an unwilled action, the other to a willed one, with the same results. 'Strangury' (p. 52), slow painful urination describes the way words appear. 'Jakes' (p. 58) is a slang word for privy or outhouse. The recurring double 'o's' of the text, supported by the double 'o' of the moon or Hecate ironically reduplicate the two holes of a typical outhouse. The phrase 'haze sole certitude' (p. 48) appears to be a parody of Verlaine's 'nuance' or Mallarmé's insistence that a poem does not tell but suggests. A most interesting example of such parody is the description of the woman eating her slop. The scene is presented with all the ritual of a mystical ceremony, including a perfect parabolic movement of systole and diastole. Earlier in the text the woman's hand movements had been described in just such terms, 'They tighten then loosen their clasp. Slow systole diastole' (p. 31). In the slop eating scene, the words are not used, but the movement is obvious:

> With her right hand as large as life she holds the edge of the bowl resting on her knees. With her left the spoon dipped in the slop. She waits. For it to cool perhaps. But no. Merely frozen again just as about to begin. At last in a twin movement full of grace she slowly raises the bowl towards her lips while at the same time with equal slowness bowing her head to join it. Having set out at the same instant they meet halfway and there come to rest. Fresh rigour before the first spoonful slobbered largely back into the slop. Others no happier till time to part lips and bowl and slowly back with never a slip to their starting points. As smooth and even fro as to. (p. 35)

The mystical experience to which such a scene would be expected to refer, is here reduced to the pedestrian, low act of eating. Furthermore the designation of the food as slop coupled with her slobbering into the slop and all the negative connotations of revulsion such words evoke further tilt the paragraph towards irony.

Beckett's transgression of the *Symbolistes'* conventions is a systematic negation of a transcendental significance assigned to the act of writing. Northrop Frye in his definition of irony views in the archetypal theme of irony 'a sense that heroism and effective action are absent, disorganized or foredoomed to defeat, and that confusion and anarchy reign over the world'.[20] In the second text of *ISIS*, that of the critical poem, the consciousness narrating comments on the 'farrago from eye to mind' (p. 40), a phrase which echoes Virginia Woolf's 'This is a farrago of absurdity'.

The second text therefore records the act of writing the 'story' of the old woman. The reader's first indication of the metafictional characteristic of this text is the recurrence of the colours white and black which colour the world of the old woman. In his essay 'Quant au livre' Mallarmé writes that 'l'homme poursuit noir sur blanc'. In his *Beckett par lui-même* Ludovic Janvier quotes Mallarmé:

> C'est un jeu insensé d'écrire, s'arroger, en vertu d'un doute—la goûte d'encre apparentée à la nuit sublime—quelque devoir de tout recréer, avec des reminiscences, pour avérer qu'on est bien là où l'on doit être (parce que permettez-moi d'exprimer cette appréhension, demeure une incertitude).[21]

Other authors have punctuated the metafictional aspect of their work with the metaphor of black and white, such as Joseph Conrad in *Under Western Skies*, but none as assiduously as Beckett. In a short text titled *Imagination Dead Imagine* white and black become the only signs of life in what appears to be a barren scene. Other indications of metafiction can be found in the questions the narrating consciousness asks itself concerning the recording of a certain scene and the answers and words of caution it gives in return. For instance while recording the area surrounding the cabin, the narrating consciousness must make such decisions as whether to include flowers, the number to use for the guardians surrounding it and their presence, 'Flowers? Careful. Alone the odd crocus still at lambing time' (p. 10). 'How many? A figure come what may. Twelve. Wherewith to furnish the horizon's narrow round. [. . .] She never once saw one coming toward her. Or she forgets. She forgets. Are they always the same? Do they see her? Enough' (p. 10). The narrative consciousness also records doubts about a choice of *locus*, 'A moor would have better met the case' (p. 11). The theme of the metafictional text is the pain of writing, the lack of certainty such an endeavour entails, and the quasi-impossibility of separating reality from fiction. A close precedent for such a polemic can be found in the poem of a post-symbolist writer Wallace Stevens. In fact there is a possibility of Beckett's alluding to Stevens's 'An Ordinary Evening in New Haven'.

> The eye's plain version is a thing apart,
> The vulgate of experience. [. . .]
> ....
> These houses, these difficult objects, dilapidate
> Appearances of what appearances,
> Words, lines, not meanings, not communications.
> ....

Reality as a thing seen by the mind,
Not that which is but that which is apprehended,

....

The objects tingle and the spectator moves
With the objects. [. . .]

....

The eye made clear of uncertainty, with the sight
Of simple seeing, without reflection. we seek
Nothing beyond reality. [. . .]

....

This endlessly elaborating poem
Displays the theory of poetry
As the life of poetry. A more severe,

More harassing master would extemporize
Subtler, more urgent proof that the theory
Of poetry is the theory of life,

As it is, in the intricate evasions of as,
In things seen and unseen, created from nothingness,
The heavens, the hells, the worlds, the longed-for lands.[22]

The numerous references to the eye in Stevens' poem parallel those of Beckett's text, the line 'In things seen and unseen', appears to have inspired the title, and Beckett might well be the 'More harassing master', who subtly gives proof that 'the theory of poetry is the theory of life'. In *ISIS* Beckett distinguishes between what the eye sees and what the mind records of what the eye sees, 'No longer anywhere to be seen. Nor by the eye of flesh nor by the other' (p. 17). When the eye is said to 'return to the scene of its betrayals' (p. 27), is it the eye of flesh which betrays 'the other' or is it the reverse? The phrase is purposefully ambiguous, in order to suggest a mutual betrayal, 'The mind betrays the treacherous eyes and the treacherous words their treacheries' (p. 48). Whose treacheries? The words' or the eyes'? As a result of the treacheries there is a confusion between what is real and what is not, only the narrative consciousness does not even have a word for the opposite of real, 'Such confusion now between real and—how say its contrary?' (p. 40) They are called 'That old tandem' (p. 40), but again there is ambiguity. Does the old tandem refer to reality and its opposite or the eye and the mind? The two 'tandems' seem to blend in what follows, 'Such confusion between them once so twain. And such the farrago from eye to mind. For it to make what sad sense of it may. No matter now. Such equal liars both. Real and—how ill say its contrary? The counterpoison' (p. 40). Just as there is no longer a difference between, say, poetry and prose, there is no longer a difference between the real and its opposite. Could it be fiction, as Borges understands it? All is fiction. Language is all that remains.

Variations of the title, as well as, at times, the title itself, recur at various times throughout the text, as though the narrative consciousness were judging the progress of the writing. This metafictional text is open-structured, linear, and temporal unlike its counterpart. It exhibits certain characteristics which Sharon Spencer attributes to an open-structured novel. It is an intellectual exploration by a writer who is not certain what he believes about reality, and it is the naked exploration of the writing process. Since it is a process it will be linear and temporal (though minimally so). This development is evident in the syntax of the metafictional text which begins rather calmly and progresses (paradoxically) toward disintegration, accompanied by a more insistent repetition of the title or variations thereof, until it arrives at a conclusion. As part of this development is the pain and difficulty of writing. There are frequent references to using the 'wrong word', and to the search for the 'sweet one word' which is compared to painful urination, 'See now how words too. A few drops mishaphazard. Then strangury' (p. 52). In the Joycean-sounding word 'mishaphazard' are contained not only the precariousness of writing but also Mallarmé's *hasard* which the latter hoped to eradicate with words. Writing is also compared to giving birth, 'quick again to the brim the old nausea and shut again. On her. Till she be whole. Or abort' (p. 38). There is also a fear of failure, 'Such—such fiasco that folly takes a hand. such bits and scraps. Seen no matter how and said as seen. Dread of black. Of white. Of void' (p. 31). When three-quarters of the way into the text the syntax begins to disintegrate, the old woman's 'story' becomes less important and the metatext takes over. It is then that the writing becomes more frantic and the pain of writing more evident. In an interesting blending of the two texts, one short strophe records both the woman's tearing of the cryptic sheet of paper she found in the old coffer and the writer's discontented destruction of his page of writing:

> The sheet. Between tips of trembling fingers. In two. Four. Eight. Old frantic fingers. Not paper any more. Each eighth apart. In two. Four. Finish with knife. Hack into shreds. Down the plughole. On to the next. White. Quick blacken. (p. 54)

The ill seen ill said have been scrapped and it is time to start again 'White. Quick blacken.' This time the quest begins behind the eye,

'Far behind the eye the quest begins' (p. 55). The mind now takes over. In Derridean terms the search for a truth outside the play of signs is a kind of exile, such as what the old woman experiences. However the acceptance of creative function, without looking back results in joy. That is why the narrative consciousness, not only tears up the ill seen ill said, but erases every trace of the old woman's 'story'.

Irony is 'a characteristic response to the polysemic world we inhabit'.[23] It is Beckett's response, who, in *ISIS*, explores the different avenues which might lead to a single answer. He finds that the *Symbolistes'* search for a transcendental principle was futile, when, as the narrative consciousness in the metatext proves, reality is just as elusive. Therefore if something apparently as simple as grasping phenomenal reality is impossible, then a transcendental principle can only be even more unattainable. What is left then is not to try to control the disconnections, the aporia, but to accept the world and its randomness and contingencies. Mallarmé thought that words could conquer '*le hasard*', Beckett knows they cannot. He is left with what Jerzy Kosinski calls happiness. 'With a true sense of the randomness of life's moments, man is at peace with himself—and that peace means happiness.'[24]. Beckett apparently agrees with Kosinski; he ends *ISIS* by revoking the text the narrative consciousness has produced.

> Farewell to farewell. Then in that perfect dark foreknell darling sound pip for end begun. First last moment. Grant only enough remain to devour all. Moment by glutton moment. Sky earth the whole kit and boodle. Not another crumb of carrion left. Lick chops and basta. No. One moment more. One last. Grace to breathe that void. Know happiness. (p. 59)

In true Beckettian fashion, the play of the signifier triumphs in the ambiguity of the last two words which cancel each other out phonetically.

READING *THAT TIME*

ANTONI LIBERA

The formal structure of the play

There are three voices marked 'A', 'B', and 'C'. Each voice tells a different story. In reality these are three monologues, parts of which are spoken alternately (analogous to *Play*). While staging the play, the author stated that Voice B narrates the story of youth; Voice C, the story of old age; and Voice A, the story of adulthood (maturity).[1]

Each voice speaks twelve times in the play, four times in each of the three parts into which the play is divided by two 10-second breaks. The formal structure of the play appears as follows:

I ACB ACB ACB CAB pause, breath
II CBA CBA CBA BCA pause, breath
III BAC BAC BAC BAC pause, smile

Clearly, there is principle at work here. The initial order of speech of the three voices, ACB, reappears for a fourth time as CAB (Voice A's lines move from the first position to the second), after which, following a pause, it again changes to CBA (Voice A's lines now move from the second to the third position). A similar shuffling occurs between parts II and III. Again after three repetitions, the initial order, CBA, changes into BCA (here Voice C's lines shift from the first to the second position). Following a pause this order changes yet again to BAC (Voice C's lines move from the second to the third position). This latter shuffling results in an order which remains unchanged to the end of the play.

These respective permutations, which always follow the same pattern, are not merely a formal game. They express the narrator's striving to order his memories, at least chronologically. Since Voice B relates the story of youth, A—adulthood, and C—old age, the order produced in part III (BAC) is, finally, correct. Thus there are no further changes and hence, among other things, the Listener's smile.

During production the author labelled the speeches of each voice in the following manner: A1, A2, A3 etc. to A12; B1, B2, B3 etc. to B12; C1, C2, C3, etc. to C12. These labels will be used in the notes which follow.[2]

The hero

The narrated stories do not lend themselves only to literal translation; they are parabolic. The protagonist of whom the three voices speak is not a real character (some concrete person) as would seem at first glance but rather a symbolic figure. In *my* interpretation, he personifies a thinking creature of European cultural background in various stages of development. Thus the situations, events and thoughts evoked present allegorical images or formulas of his spiritual adventures throughout the ages.

The symbolism of the text is not clear and does not permit unambiguous interpretation. The readings proposed below are not the only ones possible, nor necessarily the most accurate.

Voice A

The land of his childhood to which the hero returns appears to symbolize ancient Europe, especially Greece during its Golden Age. According to such an interpretation (arguments for which follow in further notes), the story of the hero's return to his homeland might reflect an event in the history of European culture like the Renaissance. In this case, Beckett presents the recollection within the play as the last return (and in the end the only one), since the period of the Renaissance was the last (and only) moment in European cultural history when man attempted to return to his roots and reestablish contact with them. Because the story of Voice A is, according to the author, the story of adulthood, the Renaissance would be the period of maturity in the history of European culture.

The essence of this period, as well as European antiquity (Greece) is described metaphorically: on the one hand, by the circumstances and course of the return; on the other hand by the evoked memories of childhood.

A 1

The day on which the protagonist arrives in his homeland is a grey day. This would suggest Autumn, all the more so since all events narrated by Voice C (the story of old age) occur in winter, and the scenes evoked by Voice B (the story of youth) occur in summer. Consequently the Renaissance was on the one hand the period of adulthood for European civilization, and on the other already its autumn.

When the hero arrives in his homeland the trams which once ran no longer exists, nor even the cables. Only the 'old rails' remain. this state of things depicts the lifelessness of old traditions and currents of thought, or at any rate their inapplicability for him who has arrived from the future. Before, he could move about freely (by tram), but as the man from the future, faced with only the tracks which remain, he can travel only with difficulty (on foot).

The question 'when was that', which is repeated twice, indicates that the problem of locating historically the attempt at a return to the roots of European culture remains an open one. Possibly this was the Renaissance, but it could have been another moment as well.

Voice C

The events evoked by Voice C (the story of old age) symbolize the spiritual adventures of European man in the last phase of his development. An analysis of the described scenes and the protagonist's thoughts which accompany them reveal allusions to transformations or breakthroughs which occurred in European culture beginning in the seventeenth or eighteenth centuries.

All events evoked by voice C take place in winter, in the rain. This means that the reality surrounding European man beginning in the seventeenth to eighteenth centuries is particularly burdensome and unfavourable, as compared to the reality he inhabited earlier. Here the unceasing rain is a symbol of the bad weather which precludes harmonious coexistence with the outside world and which forces him to take cover under various shelters of his own making (the Portrait Gallery, the Post Office, the Public Library). The only refuge for this man is the world of culture and art which he created. Except for this, all reality is unacceptable ('cold' and 'rain').

The winter mentioned is 'always winter' or as stated in C9, 'as if it couldn't end'. Such formulations testify that the cycle of seasons suffered some disruption—at least in the perception of the person remembering. Winter, instead of ending at a given moment and passing to spring, kept on and on, 'year after year'. Because the events described by Voice C are the last in the hero's story, we may assume that this final season is still continuing up to the current moment, i.e., to the moment when the person remembering recalls his past before our very eyes.

In order to understand what is meant by this we must first realize what the seasons signify in general, or rather, what they symbolize. It appears that they are cryptonyms for the three phases of historical development in the theory of history expounded by Vico. Beckett became acquainted with this theory in his youth (through Joyce) and became its adherent (traces of it can be found in many of his works).

Vico's theory maintains that humanity develops in a three-phase cycle along a spiral. These phases are: The Theocratic Age, which corresponds to the institution of Religion or to the abstraction, Birth; the Heroic Age, which corresponds to the institution of Marriage or the abstraction, Maturity; and the Human Age, corresponding to the institution of Burial or the abstraction, Corruption. After the cycle closes everything—according to Vico—begins anew, but on a higher or wider ring of the spiral: after the Human Age follows a new Divine Age which the philosopher named the Age of Divine Providence, corresponding to the abstraction, Generation.

Using Vico's theory to interpret the history of European culture, Beckett creates the following order: The Theocratic Age (symbol: summer), the epoch of great mythology, Greek and Judaeo-Christian, (the story of youth, narrated by Voice B); the Heroic Age (symbol: autumn), the apogee of the modern era, late Medieval and Renaissance, (the story of adulthood, narrated by Voice A); the Human Age (symbol: winter), the last several hundred years beginning with the seventeenth to eighteenth centuries, (the story of old age, narrated by Voice C). After this epoch, according to the theory, should follow the epoch of Divine Providence, when people themselves become gods, new gods, an era represented by abstract Generation (logically the symbol would be spring). However, in Beckett understanding this epoch has not yet come nor will it ever come. Thus the 'endless winter' symbolizes humanity (in the case of European man) stuck in the Human Age, and casts doubt on the optimistic tone of Vico's theory.

Voice B

The scenes evoked by Voice B have a different status than those evoked by Voices A and C. Inasmuch as these latter are recollections of *events*, the former consist in recollections of *dreams*. The story narrated by Voice B is thus the story of the hero's imagining certain situations, in which he does not appear as the one imagining, but as the one imagined.

The following inscription is from a director's notebook kept by the author during production of the play in Berlin:

> Alles war nun stille. Wir sprachen kein Wort,
> wir berührten uns nicht, wir sahen uns nich an . . .
>
> Hölderlin
> *Hyperion-Fragment*

As seen in the footnote this is a quotation from Friederich Hölderlin's *Hyperion-Fragment* (of a verse adaptation not to be confused with the novel *Hyperion or Eremita in Greece*). A literal translation would read: 'Now all was silent. We didn't say a word, / we didn't touch, we didn't look at one another . . .' The underlined letter B placed by the author above the quotation indicates that this fragment serves as a motto for the narration of Voice B and perhaps even as the source of inspiration for the central image.

Regardless of whether and how this main image relates to Hölderlin's poetic world, it does possess an independent meaning of its own. This image and all others derived from it form, in my opinion, a symbolic representation of that phenomenon in the history of European culture known as Judaeo-Christian Mythology. The vision of a man and woman swearing love to one another in silence is a reduction of various allegories in which man expressed his belief in the existence of a metaphysical partner, the more so since the relationship which emerges between them consists in love (the Old Testament Song of Songs, the Christian 'God is love' etc.). The behaviour of the two characters as well as circumstances accompanying their meeting express or even expose various aspects of the myth which are often not entirely obvious or are even imperceptible at first glance. Such aspects include the idea that man and God never see one another, at most they hear one another; further, that they have no physical contact; finally, that their meetings are always accompanied by fair weather and abundance. (Incidentally Hölderlin referred to the age of gods on Earth—i.e., the presence of Christ—as the 'day of the sun'.)

Furthermore, the way in which these scenes are recalled, as if they were recollections of real and not imagined events, illustrates the manner in which religious myth enters the consciousness of man, whether it be a living myth or an extinct one. Voice B's narration contains no mention of the circumstances in which the protagonist dreamt up his visions; only the visions themselves are mentioned, i.e., that they were *merely* visions and what they depicted. This suggests that the reality of myth is as powerful as, if not more powerful than, the reality of events, and that it affects human consciousness as if it were actual. In other words, the religious myth, while still alive, has the force of reality, and once extinct, has the character of history. When the hero imagined he was sitting with a woman on the stone at the edge of the little wood it was to him as if he really were sitting with her. When man truly believed in the presence of gods on Earth it was as if they were really there. (Let us recall here Beckett's sentence from his first essay *Dante . . . Bruno . . . Vico. . Joyce*: 'Jove was no symbol: he was terribly real.[2]) However, once this faith had expired, or at least had cooled significantly, that age remained present in memory (historic consciousness) just as it had been perceived before. Regardless of whether or not one believes in the divinity and resurrection of Christ, for example, the story preserved in the Gospel is much more strongly present in the consciousness of contemporary man than events related by historic chronicles.

Beckett's understanding of myth is also deeply rooted in Vico's theory.

B 2

'. . . one thing could ever bring tears . . .', i.e., one's own imagination, or, as is later stated, 'that thought', 'that scene'. Thus this one myth from among all religious myths.

A 3

'. . . bit of a tower still standing . . .' An illusion of the person remembering. During his visit the hero could not confirm in what state the tower was in because he never reached it.

'. . . she was with you then still with you . . .', i.e., in the 'kip on the front'; 'she' is the woman mentioned by Voice B. Of course, the protagonist was with her the way he was always with her, i.e., in his imagination. It follows from this that at the time of return the hero was already unable to imagine himself in the company of others. See B9.

'. . . just the one night . . .' Continuation of the question 'where did you sleep'.

'. . . in any case off the ferry one morning and back on her to the next . . .' Another illusion of the person remembering: the hero returned to the ferry the evening of that same day. See A7.

C 3

'. . . a face appeared . . .' While examining the face of some distant ancestor, the protagonist suddenly saw his own reflection in the picture-glass. However, he did not recognize his own face, and to such an extent that he turned and looked behind him suspecting it was the reflection of someone who had entered the room unnoticed and stood behind him.

This event may be interpreted in many ways. If we consider the change evoked in the hero's consciousness described in C6, we may assume that it describes a specific experience in European history, namely the discovery of the relativity of the cognitive perspective and the resultant view of history as a dialectic process. The hero's glimpsing of his own image in the image of a distant ancestor is Man's conception of his own historicity symbolically represented. It is the realization, figuratively expressed, that the perceiving subject is itself perceived and is thus equated with the object of perception. This scene is allegorical portrayal of the loss of certain attributes hitherto ascribed by man to himself, namely, superiority, independence, and immutability. This turning around to look, this act of disbelief that the face reflected is the hero's own, depicts the degree of shock caused by this degradation.

B 3

'. . . tears without fail . . .' belonging to the person imagining this scene, not the one imagined.

'. . . suddenly there in whatever thoughts you might be having whatever scenes perhaps way back . . .', i.e., the hero is moved to tears especially and exclusively by this scene, from among all his imaginings. Compare: 'one thing could ever bring tears' (B2). The 'thoughts' and 'scenes' are merely Man's early mythologies.

'. . . or that old Chinaman . . .', i.e., thoughts and scenes composed by that old Chinaman; during production the author explained that here is meant Lao Tse.

C 4

'. . . after that . . .', i.e., after what happened to the protagonist in the Portrait Gallery. See C3.

A 4

'. . . or talking to yourself . . .' Continuation of the end of A3.

'. . . loud imaginary conversations . . .' Holding loud conversations with oneself would appear to symbolize the art of dialogue invented by the Greeks. The first to write using dialogue was obstensibly Zeno of Elei; Plato perfected this style. Such an interpretation confirms the assumption made earlier that the hero's childhood symbolizes the Golden Age of ancient Greece.

B 4

'. . . or by the window in the dark harking to the owl . . .' This is not—as it might seem—the continuation of the *end* of B3, but rather of the *beginning* of that speech: 'on the stone in the sun . . .' These, as will be seen in B12, present the last of the hero's visions. This vision is fundamentally different from all the others. Here the protagonist is 'by the window', i.e., in some house, in a closed space, whereas in all the other visions he is in an open space. Further, he is 'in the dark' whereas elsewhere he is 'in the sun' or at least in the 'sunset'. Finally, instead of a *woman's* whispered declaration of love he hears the hooting of an *owl*. The owl is symbol of wisdom, of reason. Accordingly, the vision may be interpreted as a representation of the modern European myth, in which the God of Reason has replaced the God of Love.

'. . . not a thought in your head . . .' These are the few words in Voice B's text which refer to the hero as a person imagining and not as the one imagined. They describe his state of consciousness: he no longer believes in Love and cannot continue imagining the story of his meeting with a woman or even waiting for her. This story is now 'just another of those tales' as far as he is concerned. This state of the hero's imagination appears to represent the moment in European cultural consciousness when the Judaeo-Christian mythology slowly began to fade and become merely part of tradition. Historically this would be compared to the events and changes in European culture which occurred in the seventeenth and eighteenth centuries (Spinoza, Kant, Voltaire). It is significant that the author used the words 'not a thought in your head' to describe human consciousness at the time when modern myth (the myth of Reason) arose. For him this myth is thus a sign of regress more than progress.

'. . . on top of you the shroud . . .' i.e., the void. From this metaphor it follows that the void means death for the protagonist. Surrounded by the void, the hero is as if covered with a shroud, i.e., dead. Not biologically, but metaphysically. A person deprived of the mythology which offers some superior sense to his existence, which explains his origins and the purpose of his being on earth, a person incapable of either creating such mythology or believing in existing myths, such a person is exclusively a mortal being and therefore metaphysically dead.

The author recommended that the lines be spoken more slowly and quietly beginning with words 'just one of those things'. He characterized this effect by the musical term 'ritardando'.

C 5

'. . . did you ever say I to yourself in your life . . .' One of the main problems in Beckett's entire work: the questioning of the idea that Man, both as individual as well as species, is the personification of the active subject.

'. . . never but the one the first and last . . . when they lugged you out . . .' The first and only turning-point in the life of the protagonist was his birth. He now considers all other such moments as apparent turning-points.

'. . . was that the time or was that another time . . .' The beginning of the question which is finished at the start of C6: 'when you started not knowing . . . etc.', i.e., 'that time' in the Portrait Gallery.

B 5

'. . . that time . . .' These words refer not to the place and time of the tale's invention, but of the tale itself.

It is worth noting that the 'tales' take place in successively lower settings topographically in relation to sea level. The first is set as if on a plateau, the second on a river plain, the third in the dunes near the sea. This suggests that the imagined hero traverses a certain road in his

fictional world (although outside of the details concretely imagined). This road runs downhill, to the sea.

Another changing element of this picture strengthens this suggestion, namely, the position of the protagonist: at first sitting, later standing, and finally reclining. All of these details taken together give the impression of a certain evolution consisting of a downward motion on the one hand, and circular motion on the other: from one form of stasis (a sitting position) through motion (suggested by the standing position, and thus walking) to another form of immobility (reclining position). This evolution appears to represent the aging and withering away of the myth.

A 5

'. . . till the truth began to dawn . . .' The beginning of the sentence which is completed in A6: 'no getting out to it that way', i.e., the trams were no longer running.

C 6

'. . . when you started not knowing who you were from Adam. . .' Completion of the questing began at the end of C5: 'was that the time or was that another time'. The hero's loss of conviction as to the essence of his own being seems to symbolize the collapse of the belief held throughout the ages, that Man is God's child and that his stay on earth is part of an act of salvation. When biblical dogma was questioned, Man lost his metaphysical self-cognizance. Compare C3.

'. . . trying how that would work for a change . . .' This passage would logically precede the words 'when you started . . . etc.' In other words, beginning with the end of C5, the logical sequence would be 'was that the time [i.e., in the Portrait Gallery] or was that another time trying how that would work for a change not knowing who you were from Adam no notion who it was saying what you were saying whose skull you were clapped up in whose moan had you the way you were *you started* not knowing who you were from Adam'. This passage suggests that the loss of metaphysical self-cognizance was not the result of accident nor of any cataclysm, but was a *choice* born of curiosity ('trying how that would work *for a change*'). The passage is also a specific reference to the myth of original sin: the price of knowledge is expulsion from Paradise, in this case being the religious system which offers sense, hope and security.

'. . . whose moan had you the way you were . . .', i.e., the agony of Christ as the foundation of Christianity which formed modern European culture.

'. . . not believing it could be you . . .', i.e., that the reflection on the picture-glass is the protagonist's own. This passage suggests that the collapse of metaphysical self-cognizance began when the immurability of human cognitive perspective was first questioned. Compare C3.

A 6

'. . . Doric terminus of the Great Southern and Eastern . . .' A further allusion to ancient Greece as the land of childhood to which the protagonist is returning.

C 7

'. . . trying making it up that way . . .', i.e., the way in which the protagonist always imagined himself, by creating himself through the invention and eventual acceptance of continually new ideas about his own existence.

'. . . how it would work that way for a change never having been . . .' Logically this passage should precede 'trying making it up that way as you went along'. Compare C6. The words 'never having been' refers to existential being (i.e., specific, human existence conscious of itself) and not ontological (general) being.

'. . . trying to wangle you into it . . .', i.e., an object and not a subject, a thing and not a being. The hero's abandonment of the conviction he has hitherto held, namely, that he is a person ('you'), and his acknowledgement that he is an 'it' appears to symbolize the origin and dissemination of certain materialistic concepts which reify the human being. The prime example of such concepts is Marxism.

'. . . all over the parish . . .', i.e., through *that* sphere of culture which is Europe.

B 7

'. . . wherever it was . . .', whether 'on the stone at the edge of the little wood', or 'on the towpath', or 'in the sand'.

A 7

'. . . gave it up gave up . . .' The answer to the question in the end of A6: 'so what next'.

'. . . for it to be time to get on the night ferry . . .' Here the protagonist recalls when he actually finished his visit to his home town. Compare A3.

'. . . the passers pausing to gape at you quick gape then pass pass on pass by on the other side . . .' During production the author stated that this image constitutes a distant echo of a certain scene in the Gospel according to Luke. However, he did not explain exactly which scene was meant. There are two possibilities: either Jesus' parable of the good Samaritan: 'A certain man went down from Jerusalem to Jericho, and fell among thieves, which stripped him of his raiment, and wounded him, and departed, leaving him half dead. And by chance there came down a certain priest that way: and when he saw him, he *passed by on the other side*. And likewise a Levite, when he was at the place, came and looked on him, and *passed by on the other side*.' (Luke 10: 30-32); or the scene before the cross: 'And the people stood beholding' (Luke, 23:35). This second scene also evokes the well-known 22nd Psalm, especially verses 13 and 17: 'They gaped upon me with their mouths', 'they look and stare upon me'.

B 8

'. . . in the sun then sink and vanish . . .' Apart from displaying a certain evolution in regard to the setting and position of the protagonist (see B5), the scenes evoked by Voice B also change in regard to the time of day or the position of the sun. The scene on the stone always takes place under full sun; similarly, the scene on the towpath occurs as the sun is setting. The last scene ('by the window') happens at night, in the dark.

C 8

'. . . great thing free culture far from home . . .' A metaphor for the role of humanistic culture during European Man's final stage of development, and at the same time a portrayal of his own situation. European Man, according to this metaphor, is homeless ('far from home') exiled, has been disinherited and must pay for everything (figuratively speaking). His only refuge is the world of art (the Portrait Gallery) or ideas (the library), neither of which has any practical application. The world (of art and ideas) has replaced his home, his earlier religious mythology. Compare note on Voice C.

A 8

'. . . place might have been uninhabited . . .' Here the hero once again becomes the child, a person for whom loneliness is especially painful and who easily feels lonely. This experience seems to refer to the moment immediately following the Renaissance, that fruitless return to antiquity. The fact that the protagonist did not reach the ruins where he hid as a child (Plato's cave?), and that he stopped somewhere along the road, at the Doric terminus (ancient Rome?) indicates that the link to one of major sources of European culture (ancient Greece) was only half established and in essence was unsuccessful. At the same time the attempt was strong enough to restore currency to several essential questions, and thus bring Man back to a certain starting-point.

B 9

'. . . or alone in the same the same scenes . . .', i.e., on the stone at the edge of the little wood, or on the towpath, or in the sand—the hero alone without the woman.

'. . . making it up that way . . .', i.e., without the woman.

'. . . to keep it going to keep it [void] out . . .' The reason for inventing these scenes. Compare B4.

C 9

'. . . always winter then endless winter year after year . . .' This formulation indicates clearly that the word 'winter' is used figuratively and not literally. Compare note on Voice C.

'. . . that time in the Post Office all bustle Christmas bustle . . .' It is difficult to state exactly what historical moment is meant. However, based on what follows as well as on distinctive details ('with all the forms and the pens on their chains'), we may assume that the Post Office symbolizes comtemporary, highly organized consumer society.

The words 'bustle', 'Christmas bustle', as well as 'forms' and 'pens on their chains' already mentioned, characterize the nature of this society: motion, the unceasing pursuit of something, and at the same time bureaucracy and ever-present formalities.

B 10

'. . . an earlier time a later time before she came after she went or both before she came after she was gone . . .' These questions imply that, before he imagined himself in the company of a woman, the hero imagined himself alone, and that this vision coincides with the one he had *after* he ceased imagining himself with a woman. Thus he first imagined himself as waiting for someone, next as in someone's company, and finally as abandoned by someone. These three types of imagination appear to correspond to three forms of the Judaeo-Christian myth: waiting for the Messiah (Old Testament), his presence on earth (the Gospels), his departure and Man's waiting once more for his return (history of Christianity).

'. . . that time in the sand the glider passing over . . .' The glider indicates that this vision must have originated at a time when such an object already existed, thus in the twentieth century. This observation explains the two corrections of the speaking voice ('soon after long after') following the mistaken attempt to locate this scene at the time of the hero's return ('that time you went back') to his home town, which represents—as we have assumed—the Renaissance.

A 10

'. . . you heard yourself at it again . . .', i.e., muttering to himself again.

C 10

'. . . till it dawned that for all the loathing you were getting you might as well not have been there at all the eyes passing over you and through you like so much thin air . . .' At this moment the protagonist observed that other people really didn't notice him and that his presence at the Post Office meant absolutely nothing. This experience seems to symbolize the reduction of the individual to an annoymous changeable part. It expresses one of the fundamental contradictions of highly organised contemporary civilization; nominally it serves the individual, having been created to satisfy his needs—in fact, it reduces him to a statistical unit, renders him insignificant, superfluous, and replaceable.

'. . . or was that another time another place another time . . .' These questions indicate that the problem of locating the above experience historically remains unsolved.

B 11

'. . . in the great peace like a whisper so faint she loved you hard to believe you even you made up that bit . . .' As mentioned in note to B 10, the glider flying overhead implies that this scene occurred in the twentieth century, which is characterised by hitherto unheard of cruelties and cataclysms. These events were so tremendous as to challenge the belief that 'God is love'. At the same time twentieth century Man preserved this belief—at least to some extent. This is expressed in the words 'you even you [twentieth century Man] made up that bit' (that you are still with 'her'—i.e., God, and that God still loves you). The specified passage might be translated: it's really inconceivable that twentieth century Man, who has experienced such terrible disasters (afflictions), has gone through so many hells and who is lonely and abandoned as never before still is able to believe that God loves him.

A 11

'. . . making yourself all up again for the millionth time . . .', i.e., inventing some new anthropological theory.

C 11

'. . . the Library that was another place another time . . .' Continuation of the C 10.

B 12

'. . . that time in the end when you tried and couldn't . . .', i.e., making it (stories, tales) up any more. Connects to the last imagined story, mentioned first time in B4.

'. . . and the owl flown to hoot at someone else . . .' A symbolic, also ironic representation of the collapse of the myth, in which the God of Reason was Man's partner.

'. . . not a sound . . ., i.e., from any divine being.

'. . . when you tried and tried and couldn't any more. . ' The death of Man's ability to invent myth.

'. . . no words left to keep it out . . .' It = the void. Compare B9.

'. . . a great shroud . . .', again, the void. See B4.

'. . . and little or nothing the worse little or nothing . . .' The decline of the last myths and Man's finding himself in a void was not as great a shock as he feared. He passed from a period of coexistence with the gods to a point where they abandoned him, and this passage proved unexpectedly mild, almost unnoticeable. This was nonetheless a passage of fundamental significance, thus the correction 'little or nothing'.

A 12

'. . . was there ever any other time but that time . . .' Man's return to his roots, to the roots of European culture, whenever it occurred, occurred only once.

C 12

'. . . only what was it it said . . .', i.e., what the dust said.

'. . . come and gone . . .' At first, the person recalling these scenes believes that the dust said 'come and gone'. However, after testing his memory by twice repeating these words he discards this hypothesis. He then maintains the dust said: 'no one come and gone'. However, he corrects this immediately and offers a third version: 'in no time gone'. This is the correct version, and he repeats it to confirm it.

The scene in the Library, when the protagonist hears the dust speak, seems to illustrate our current moment in history, when Man is confronted by nothingness at the centre of a civilisation which appears to be the exact opposite of nothingness. In earlier times Man heard himself, or—in his imagination—the voice of a woman, or if necessary an owl; now he hears only the voice of dust, a synonym of nothingness. The God of Dialogue (childhood, ancient Greece) was replaced in time by the God of Love (youth, Christianity), which in turn gave way in time to the God of Reason (maturity, Enlightenment:

rationalism and materialism). Finally the God of Nothingness (old age, twentieth century, atheism) replaced the God of Reason. The words spoken by the dust express with forceful brevity the essence of contemporary consciousness: the disbelief in the supernatural and the resultant feeling that everything is crumbling and about to vanish. The words 'come and gone' seem to refer to the individual human being as well as to the entire, age-old human culture. The only truth for contemporary Man is transience, impermanence, decay. People and entire cultures are born and die ('come and gone') and nothing of them remains, and there is no sense in these events. Their life is wearisome, exhausting, and when it finally ends, it seems to have been but an instant ('in no time gone').

THE SPEECH ACT IN BECKETT'S *OHIO IMPROMPTU*

KATHLEEN O'GORMAN

The Issues

In Samuel Beckett's play, *Ohio Impromptu* (1981), a Listener and a Reader, closely resembling one another, sit at a table—the former facing the audience, the latter at a right angle to him facing centre stage, both with heads bowed. The Reader reads from a book on the table in front of him, occasionally interrupted by a knock on the table by the Listener. Whenever the Listener knocks, the Reader repeats the last segment of what he has just read and continues with what follows. At one point the Listener stops the Reader from turning back to an earlier page to which the text refers, and at another the Reader pauses at an ungrammatical structure in the text, says, 'Yes', and re-reads it. After finishing the book, Reader closes it, and Reader and Listener raise their heads and look at one another for the first time. The lights fade after ten seconds, and the play has finished.

There seems to be nothing especially noteworthy about the sequence of events which comprises *Ohio Impromptu*, and yet the drama is quite compelling. What, then, of the text which the Reader reads? Does it somehow provide the dramatic impetus of the play? The narrative, written in the past tense, tells the story of a man who has left his beloved and who regrets his 'error'.[1] He sees no hope of turning back and remains instead on the Isle of Swans, to which he has retreated. He has spent his days pacing the island in his long, black coat and Latin Quarter hat, seeking 'some measure of relief'.[2] His dreams are troubled, and his old terror of night returns. One night, a man appears to him who says he was sent by 'the dear one'. This man reads to the first through the night and returns to do so regularly, until one night he says he will not return. The two 'sat on as though turned to stone'.[3]

While this may or may not be an absorbing tale, I think it fairly safe to say that on its own the story hardly seems sufficient to provide any significant dramatic momentum to the play. Yet if neither the external events nor the embedded text give *Ohio Impromptu* its impact, how are we to account for it as drama, as performance? We need to ask ourselves two questions: (1) What exactly happens in the play? and (2) How does it happen?

The answer to the first emerges in a consideration of the relationships which develop among the various elements of the play. For most critics, 'what happens' centres on the issue of identity: as Reader's text affirms, 'With never a word exchanged they grew to be as one'.[4] This growing to be as one comes to determine what happens on a number of different levels: to the two characters in the text, to the Reader and Listener on stage, to the characters on stage as they relate to those in the text, and, finally, to the narrative and dramatic texts. A brief sampling of critical opinion will establish the terms in which the play has been discussed.

Yosumari Takahashi states that in *Ohio Impromptu* 'it is suggested that Listener and Reader are, despite their separate identities, those halves of a split self that we are by now familiar with'[5] in Beckett's drama and contends further that 'what Reader reads from the book is *clearly* a story of Listener's life'.[6] Henry Popkin agrees: after describing the events of the narrative which the Reader reads, Popkin affirms, '*obviously* it is this message, this book, and this reading [which are read about] which we observe on stage'.[7] Charles Lyons details more of the subtleties of the play than the others, yet he, too, states that '[a]s the reader proceeds with the narrative that tells the story of the grieving man and his nocturnal visitor, the audience assumes that these two figures [on stage] are identical with their fictional or textual counterparts'.[8] Ruby Cohn recognizes this coalescence of identities yet acknowledges as well their divergence: 'On stage the refracted images of old men resonate towards reflection within the tale that is read from the book. . . . Within the book-tale, however, the two men "grew to be as one" as the tale is repeatedly read, while on stage the two men diverge before our eyes'.[9] Stanley Gontarski's tentativeness when confronted with the central issue of identity in the play betrays itself in his introduction and elimination of important qualifiers in different versions of his review of the original production of *Ohio Impromptu*. 'Reader reads a narrative featuring a protagonist who is *evidently* a younger version of Listener';[10] 'A man (*perhaps* the Reader before us, who is visually an alter ego) . . . reads to the protagonist through the night an account of what we roughly witness on stage for the play's duration, but not exactly';[11] 'Through these meetings "they grew to be as one"—*if ever they were other*—a unity reinforced tropologically by the single hat that sits on the table'.[12]

I will return later to Cohn's and Gontarski's important modifications in their readings of *Ohio Impromptu*; I would like to begin, instead, by drawing attention to those features they share with the majority of critics who have written about *Ohio Impromptu*. What all accept—explicitly or otherwise—is that the relationship between the text read and the dramatic scene witnessed by the audience generates the central dramatic issue of the play: that of identity and difference. What most affirm is the convergence of identities which takes place between the Reader on stage and his counterpart in the text read and between the Listener on stage and the grieving man described in the text. They acknowledge then implicitly that such identification extends further: that Reader and Listener in the text come to be as one; that the Reader and Listener on stage do the same; and that the text read and the drama witnessed share a single identity, if an identity somewhat confounded by the notion of time.

Accepting for the moment that those identifications do indeed take place, we need to focus more closely on the statement which generates these transformations and which provides the play with its dramatic force. 'With never a word exchanged they grew to be as one.' What gives an utterance of this sort the capacity to effect such changes—to *do* something rather than merely say something? Different ways of framing the question would doubtless lead to different readings of the play, but the strategy which suggests to me the most compelling and provocative of formulations and which accounts for the difficulties of the play as well is that offered by speech act theory. Because speech act theory considers language in terms of performance—its capacity to do things—and because Beckett so radically diminishes the non-verbal action in his more recent plays and relies instead on the spoken word for dramatic effect, the two seem especially suited to one another. Before I examine the play in greater detail, then, let me review briefly what speech act theory entails.

Speech Acts

In trying to determine when and how words go beyond merely saying something and actually do something, Oxford philosopher John L. Austin formulated a number of considerations which seemed to him—and still do to speech act theorists—to embody the central concerns at issue. Austin posited the difference in terms of 'constatives'[13]—words which say something, like 'Paris is the capital of France'[14]—and 'performatives'[15]—words which actually do something, like my decreeing 'Paris is the capital of France' if I am the person authorised to decide which city will be the capital, if the situation meets the necessary conditions for my pronouncement to be binding, etc. As this example illustrates, by the way, no specific vocabulary and no grammatical criteria adequately differentiate between constative and performative utterances. The two statements I choose to illustrate the different kinds of utterance use exactly the same words and have identical grammatical constructions. As Austin recognised early in his deliberations, then, we need to consider all aspects of the situation in which an utterance occurs to determine its force as a performative. Austin dismissed what he termed the 'true/false fetish'[16] regarding performatives and substituted for it the 'doctrine of Infelicities',[17] or the success criterion: that is, the consideration of whether or not a performative actually achieves its purpose.

As his work continued, Austin found the constative—performative distinction problematic and ultimately abandoned it for a broader definition of performative which came to include constatives. In short, he came to view all utterances as performative, as speech acts. To take the example of the constative utterance, 'Paris is the capital of France', Austin would conclude that the speaking of the words still performs an action: it makes an assertion, establishes a position. To account for the apparent difference between that kind of activity and the kind performed in the act of decreeing Paris to be the capital of France, Austin isolates the notion of the force of an utterance and determines three distinct acts involved in the issuing of an utterance which provide ways of talking about what happens in the act of speaking. Those acts he terms (1) the locutionary—'roughly equivalent to "Meaning" in the traditional sense'; (2) the illocutionary—'such as informing, ordering, warning, undertaking, etc., i.e. utterances which have certain (conventional) force'; and (3) perlocutionary—'what we bring about or achieve *by* saying something, such as convincing, persuading, deterring . . .'.[18] Austin then classifies utterances according to their illocutionary force—a classification which he suggests himself is tentative and which later speech act theorists, notably John Searle,[19] have revised and refined.

In shifting their emphasis from the constative—performative distinction and concentrating instead on the notion of the illocutionary force of an utterance, Austin, Searle, and those who have followed attempt to identify those elements in the speech situation which affect the impact utterances can have, rather than focusing on their meaning, on the locutionary act. That will be my emphasis as well in examining what happens in *Ohio Impromptu*.

Text and Context

If we accept Austin and Searle's frame of reference to elucidate what I have identified as the central speech act in *Ohio Impromptu*, we accept as well the notion that no particular vocabulary or grammatical structures determine the illocutionary force of an utterance, that nothing inherent in the utterance generates its performative capacity. At this point, it is important to bear in mind that speech act theory is context-based; that is, the illocutionary force of an utterance is bound to the situation in which that utterance is issued and depends on a wide range of phenomena for its true impact. To paraphrase one of Austin's examples, my reciting the words 'I do' when asked if I take this person to be my lawful wedded spouse has very different consequences if I am reciting lines in a play as opposed to reciting them in a church, in the presence of a minister and witnesses, etc. 'We must', as Austin says, 'consider the total situation in which the utterance is issued—the total speech act'.[20]

What, then, is the context which given the utterance 'With never a word exchanged they grew to be as one' the force to effect a change in the relationship between the two characters on stage with one another and with the two characters in the text read, as well as between the text read and the drama witnessed? What are the conditions necessary and sufficient for those changes to occur?

The Reader's text in which the utterance occurs suggests identity beyond the single statement I have isolated for study. Almost identical words, 'seen the dear face and heard the unspoken words',[21] and later, 'I saw the dear face and heard the unspoken words'[22] are attributed initially to the grieving man and subsequently to his nocturnal visitor. Clearly the intimacy one shares with 'the dear one' is the same as the other's—in kind if not in fact. That the visitor 'appears' and 'disappears' suggests that he may be a projection of the grieving man's need for comfort and not a separate, vital entity at all. Likewise, the anonymity of the characters in the text and those on stage allows more readily for the convergence of their identities. (In the original manuscript, Beckett has the grieving man addressed at one point as '[Aloysius] Mortimer' but later decided against such specificity, despite the striking aptness of the name.) These textual references alone, however, are not sufficient to empower a single utterance with the capacity to transform so many and such varied relationships. The drama of which that narrative forms an integral part must somehow substantiate the claims of the embedded text. It does so primarily through resemblance to that text.

The narrative details the presence of two men: one who listens and another who reads to him. While it refers to a third person—'the dear one'—that person is an absence and never appears in the tale except as such. Likewise on stage the audience is presented with two men only: one who listens and another one who reads to him. The number of men on stage must necessarily correspond with that in the narrative if the ambiguous 'they' is to have effect: a single reader reading to himself or a listener listening to a disembodied voice would destroy the ambiguity of the pronoun and the force of the simile, 'they grew to be *as* one' (emphasis mine). More than two characters on stage would unnecessarily confound the possible identification on all of the levels on which it takes place, upsetting the duality crucial to the notion of the narrative and dramatic texts growing to be as one.

Beyond that, the two characters on stage must resemble one another physically as closely as possible; otherwise, their growing to be as one would be frustrated visually and the possibility of change occurring in their relationship would be diminished radically, if not ultimately defeated. Beckett anticipates this need, specifying in his preliminary stage directions that the two characters on stage are to be dressed identically and are both to have long, white hair. He stated explicitly that they should be '[a]s alike in appearance as possible'.[23] While it is necessary for Reader and Listener to resemble one another, that resemblance alone does not suffice to allow for their possible identification with the characters in the text read. It is of vital importance that they resemble as well the characters described in the narrative. Reader reads of the man seeking some measure of relief who could be seen every day '[i]n his long black coat no matter what the weather and old world Latin Quarter hat'.[24] The man who comes to read to him also wears a long, black coat, according to the text. Again Beckett's initial stage directions specifically provide for the convergence of one set of characters with the other, indicating that Reader and Listener both wear long, black coats. On the table in front of them is a single black, wide-brimmed hat: an old world Latin Quarter hat. Visually, then, at *least*, the pair are 'alter egos',[25] and potentially that pairing extends to—or from—their relationship with the characters in the narrative which Reader reads.

For the force of the utterance, 'With never a word exchanged they grew to be as one', to have effect—or even potential—are the number and physical resemblance of characters on stage with one another and with those in the narrative text sufficient? If, for example, the characters on stage were to dress and appear as specified and carried on discussions about the text which the Reader reads, would such a pronouncement affect them in the same way in which it does? Clearly it could not: the possibility of the utterance's being self-referential would be invalidated by their exchanging words. A further necessary condition, then, determined by the word 'never' in the embedded text, is that the Listener and Reader on stage do not actually exchange words with one another. Technically, this condition is fulfilled by the Reader's refusal to speak at all. Though Reader reads and Listener communicates by knocking on a table, they never do 'exchange' words.

Several other details contribute to the illocutionary force of the utterance in effecting the identification on all levels, but they are neither necessary nor sufficient to enable that identification to take place. The presence of a physical text from which the Reader reads suggests that to which the narrative alludes, and the positioning of the Listener and Reader in identical poses forming 'refracted images'[26] suggests some possible relationship. In addition, the diminution of non-verbal acts helps focus attention on the speech act and concentrates its effectiveness. I mention these in the interest of making the context as fully explicit as possible, not to put undue emphasis on their importance.

Three other important considerations, though, need to be brought to bear on our determination of the context which gives force on this utterance. The first is that the old man seeking comfort and the reader who shows up one day to read 'the sad tale'[27] and who returns continuously are both presented as part of a text—the narrative which the Reader on stage reads. That is to say, they belong in a context of their own—a context which is revealed only through the Reader's words and so does not, strictly speaking, exist in three-dimensional form for Reader or audience. The context described includes physical characteristics—an unfamiliar room with a single window on the far bank of the Isle of Swans—and psychological factors—a broken relationship with a beloved, dreams, terrors, the passage of time, and a meditation on the relationship which develops between the grieving man and his nocturnal visitor. But the context is revealed exclusively through language and is thus limited in its realization, if boundless in its potential. As a narrative written in the past tense, the story is presented neither as fact nor as fiction; it is simply read. Its mode of discourse gives it an identity of its own as a text, and yet that identity blurs considerably if it does not change outright when the Reader reads, 'With never a word exchanged they grew to be as one'. In effect, a statement within the text alters that which is external to it.

To understand how, we must consider that the narrative itself occurs within a larger context: it forms part of the dramatic situation in which the characters on stage relate to one another. In fact, it constitutes the primary means of communication between the two, and as such assumes a much greater importance than it might otherwise have. But in what exactly consists the relationship between the narrative and the dramatic texts? To what extent do text and context determine one another? In *Ohio Impromptu*, the narrative read and the context of the drama in which it is read depend heavily on one another, as the narrative supplies all but one word of the discourse of the play. 'Yes',[28] suggests the Reader is affirming that he has read correctly the awkward grammatical construction immediately preceding. More importantly, he is clearly questioning the accuracy of that construction, rather than simply reading meaningless words. In effect, his one 'impromptu' remark—and I recognize that as part of the prescribed dramatic text the word 'impromptu' is a relative term—constitutes a 'metanarrative'[29] which to some extent calls into question the embedded narrative. While the embedded text thus threatens to usurp the authority of the dramatic text by supplying the primary discourse of the play, the fact of the Reader's manipulation of that text undercuts its ultimate authority. In addition to his questioning the grammatical construction of part of the narrative, Reader's frequent repetitions of passages of the narrative in response to Listener's knocks on the table establish some measure of independence from that text from the outset. Reader's first words, 'Little is left to tell. In a last—'[30] are interrupted by a knock which compels him to pause, repeat his words, and continue. As much as anything else, that first knock by the Listener and Reader's response to it determine early on in the course of events the play of authority between the narrative and dramatic texts.[31] That in turn establishes their independence from one another as text and context vie with each other for primacy.

Acknowledging that opposition, we cannot ignore the extent to which the words of the narrative text coincide with the discourse of the dramatic one. Except for the word 'yes' already cited and the Reader's repetitions of segments of what he reads, the two are identical. This identity intensifies the illocutionary force of the utterance, 'With never a word exchanged they grew to be as one', by allowing for the possibility that 'they' could refer to narrative text and dramatic context as well as to the different characters on stage and described in the reading. This convergence of aural with visual, of text with context—or at least the problematics of their effect on one another—serves as a paradigm of the change in relationship made possible by the utterance. Such a paradigm itself subverts the authority of text and of context, destroying any illusion of hierarchic relation and replacing it with one of mutual determination.

Finally, the narrative text and the drama in which it figures so prominently compel a recognition beyond the bounds of the action taking place on stage: they occur within a context we can easily take for granted and which goes by the name of 'theatre'. A reminder of the difference that makes may help elucidate the most dynamic if evasive of contextual factors which gives the speech act its illocutionary force. To see two men dressed alike and resembling one another sitting in a room, one reading while the other responds by knocking on a table would, under most circumstances, perhaps seem peculiar. If we could hear the text being read and heard exactly what the script calls for in *Ohio Impromptu*, we would not be much enlightened and, depending on our reason for listening in the first place, would probably just shrug our shoulders and go on our way. But to consent to the condition of the theatre—to take on the role of audience at a play—is to become part of a larger situation, part of what John Searle terms an 'extra-linguistic situation', which 'confer[s] status in a way relevant to illocutionary force'.[32] Petr Bogatyrev argues convincingly that the stage 'radically transforms all objects and bodies defined within it, bestowing upon them overriding signifying power . . . which is not at least evident in their normal social functions'.[33] Such a transformation depends on the audience's recognizing a performance as such, framing the drama cognitively and accepting that 'an alternative and fictional reality is to be presented'.[34]

As members of an audience, 'we knowingly and willingly enter a speech situation in which another speaker [or speakers] has unique access to the floor',[35] but as members of an audience attending a play, we clearly do much more than that. Keir Elam, in *The Semiotics of Theatre and Drama*, makes several pertinent observations.[36] The first is that the audience actively involves itself in 'constructing' the dramatic world by interpreting and making cohere the 'physical "sayings"' on stage and the fragments of spatial and temporal reference which the drama supplies. In *Ohio Impromptu*, Beckett exploits his audience's impulse to impose order on the fragments with which it is presented by offering visual and auditory versions of hypothetical worlds which may or may not coincide with one another.

He leaves it to the audience to determine for itself the extent to which those worlds are identical. In describing dramatic worlds as conjectural, 'as if' constructs,[37] Elam identifies one of the most significant factors which intensify the illocutionary force of the speech act in *Ohio Impromptu*. The audience's acceptance of the hypothetical as if it were actual in the dramatic situation itself predisposes them to accept the figurative, 'they grew to be as one', literally. The audience, then, attributes to the utterance its true illocutionary force[38]—receives and confers signification—though it may not even be aware that it is doing so.[39] Text and context, then, depend on one another in the most subtle and complex of ways, and that mutual determination gives drama in general and *Ohio Impromptu* in particular much of their vitality.

Felicity or Infelicity

I promised to return to the important modifications Ruby Cohn and Stanley Gontarski have made in their discussions of the issue of identification in *Ohio Impromptu*. I return to those modifications prepared to acknowledge that—after all this!—the convergence of characters and of texts with their various counterparts may not occur in the play. The absolute identification of one with the other is never fully realized on any level. The utterance itself, 'With never a word exchanged they grew to be as one', invites equivocal readings, with its unclear pronoun reference, 'they', and its use of simile to suggest relation rather than literal statement to designate identity. The effect is to establish simultaneously the convergence and divergence of the various elements of the drama, an effect reinforced by other manifestations of the relation of singularity to duality throughout the play. These include the notion of the couple's being 'alone together'[40] juxtaposed to the grieving man's being 'him[self] alone';[41] the image of the stream, 'How in joyous eddies its two arms conflowed and flowed united on';[42] and the doubling of the single text through repetition of many of its parts, in tandem as well as at a remove from one another. The most striking instance of this last is the immediate repetition of the first line of the narrative, 'Little is left to tell',[43] and its recurrence approximately half way through the play; its repetition twice with one word altered, 'Nothing is left to tell'[44] to close the play, again draws attention to the issue of identity and difference. The text retains singularity while doubling itself in a different way as well. There is always only one book on the table from which the Reader reads—one text—but that text becomes another as it defines the discourse of the drama. Beyond that, as Cohn and Gontarski indicate, the final visual image of the characters on stage, heads raised, looking at one another, 'suggests more mindfulness than mindlessness'[45]—contravenes, therefore, the final verbal description in the text.

What, then, of this speech act which may or may not do something, may or may not perform such transformations? What of all the textual and contextual considerations to determine the illocutionary force of the utterance? To conclude that the utterance does nothing would involve more than simply rejecting the basic tenet of speech act theory which considers all utterance to be performative. It would also radically diminish the potential of language in drama and in all discourse, and, regarding *Ohio Impromptu*, would minimize the importance of what most critics and audiences have identified as the central issue of the play. A more felicitous solution—and I use Austin's term here deliberately—is to recognize that what the utterance does may be something slightly different from, yet compatible with, what we have thus far considered. 'With never a word exchanged they grews to be as one' finally posits relationship, without definitively affirming or denying the fulfilment of that for which it allows. The utterance sets in motion a dialectic of identity and difference in which the similarity of the opposing forces—sight/sound, narrative/dramatic, presence/absence, singularity/duality—sustains as well as a dialectic of authority. In the end, neither element in any of the pairings prevails; they continuously vie for primacy, giving a dynamic movement to the play which it would otherwise lack. The illocutionary force of the speech act in *Ohio Impromptu* compels the audience to confer signification, even as it resists such a gesture.

Just as the drama refuses to yield to a single solution, resists finally the notion of identity which it so forcefully proposes, so the play's title affirms and denies simultaneously that which it offers. As Stanley Gontarski suggests, *Ohio Impromptu* is a 'straightforwardly descriptive' title, 'marking occasion and genre—impromptus à la Molière and Giraudoux (which were metatheatrical or self-reflexive exercises)—or more like the intricate little solo pieces Schubert, Chopin, and Schumann called impromptus'.[46] The Reader makes a remark not written in the text from which he reads ('Yes')[47] and repeats passages of the narrative when Listener knocks on the table, but, again to quote Gontarski, '[t]he words are already engraven—in the larger text',[48] that of the play. We do Beckett and the play no favour trying to validate the play's status as an impromptu while ignoring the contradictions inherent in such a title and paying no heed to our own experience of the drama as a highly regulated presentation. In promising an impromptu—a performance without preparation—the title of the play subverts its own promise when followed by a text which allows for no extemporaneous composition, no improvisation on the part of the actors. *Ohio Impromptu* is as carefully contrived a spectacle and as precise and unspontaneous a presentation as Beckett could detail. From the initial verbal gesture of the play—its title—through its final sustaining of binary oppositions, then, Beckett exploits fully the textual and contextual elements which give illocutionary force to language and dialectical energy to drama. He creates in the process an artifact at once straightforward and subversive, compelling yet resistant.

'MAKE SENSE WHO MAY', A STUDY OF *CATASTROPHE* AND *WHAT WHERE*

ANNAMARIA SPORTELLI

Les relations signifiantes du language artistique sont à découvrire a *l'interieur* d'une composition. L'art n'est jamais ici qu'une oeuvre d'art particuliere, où l'artiste instaure librement des opposition et des valeurs dont il joue en toute souveraineté, ne ayant ni de 'réponse' à attendre, ni de contradiction à eliminer, mais seulement une vision à exprimer selon des critères, conscients ou non dont la composition entière porte témoignage et devient manifestation.

(Benveniste: *Problèmes de linguistique générale 2*)[1]

My concern in these pages has been less to analyse Samuel Beckett's later plays *Catastrophe* and *What Where* than to enucleate catastrophe as the hidden *morphé* of Beckett's plays, i.e. as the dynamic 'projectual' form proceding along the temporal co-ordinate, which underlies and generates the spatial configuration and the consequent transformations of his dramatic 'corpus'.

Although each of the plays examined exploits different configuration, no temporal development emerges; the *morphé* in fact is never to be assumed as a diachronic system relying on continuity, but rather as a process undoing the sequel and recodifying the new.

The Greek root of the word 'catastrophe', *katastrefein*, to overturn, makes configuration and transformation implicit to the reference system. Obviously the understanding of its mechanisms (morphogenesis) and of its modalities (morphology) would call for special attention although it is the former which is at play here: that is the gradual bringing to light of 'how' the underlying structure comes to assume a form, of 'how' the structured conflict emerges, for example, since the first lines of Beckett's essay on Proust (1929):

The Proustian equation is never simple. The unknown, choosing its weapons from a hoard of values, is also unknowable.[2]

Here the critical notation is given immediate dignity of abstraction through the analogical process, that is through the reference to a stronger system of generalization. Equation, in fact, unlike identification, is verifiable only through special values ('a hoard of values') given to its variant ('the unknown'). The solution to it may be either finite or infinite and *the search* itself ('the Proustian demonstration') *is the solution* of the equation considered.

Consequently, being any solution in a broad sense the result of a conflictual game of inclusions and exclusions, if the search is the solution, *the search is the conflict*. So the conflict becomes the cipher of a process which undoes, 'interrupts (disfigures)'[3] the *continuum* to recodify it up to a new point of *disfazione*: 'Leonardo knows, when he speaks of *disfazione* that for him no one fragment will be lost'[4].

In the genesis of forms each fragment becomes the generative propulsor of any new 'adaptation' after each 'calamitous[5] and even Beckett's attempt to mime insisted circularity, indeed endless redundance up to phantasmatic disappearance, is but his way to 'geometrize' ('the sacred ruler and compass of literary geometry')[6] to redefine the new process in space-time dimension.

Meantime Beckett's formal expression records the points of *disfazione*, the inverted apex of catastrophe, as 'abrasions' on the chain of meaning, so that the problem remains of how one may accede not only to the 'dislocation' of Beckett's cosmography, but also to the textual displacement and to the discontinuity of his dramatic language. In his theoretical assumption Beckett seems to offer a key to the reading of the discontinuous when he states that

> The periods of transition that separate consecutive adaptations (because by no expedient of macabre transubstantiation can the grave-sheets serve as swaddling-clothes) represents the perilous zones in the life of the individual, dangerous, precarious, mysterious and fertile, when for a moment the boredom of living is replaced by the suffering of being.[7]

where he answers the question of how to master discontinuity, not surely bridging the abyss through potential hysotopies apt to reconstruct wholeness, but rather investigating within the abyss 'dangerous, precarious, mysterious and fertile'. Thus all tensions at play move beyond the visible and the seizable, towards those 'perilous zones' where the organic microcosm unveils itself in its swarming existence.

In recent years the scientific debate has been often concerned with the difficult principle of discontinuity. Concentrating on the evidence of the instability and potential transformations of a system, it has elaborated the Catastrophe Theory which is, in the words of its proponent René Thom, 'a methodology more than a theory in the proper sense'. The excursus inside the strictly scientific method, proposed here, is meant to be of some help for the understanding of the genesis of forms *a l'interieur* of Beckett's dramatic production.

In the broad field of the study of both natural and cultural phenomena, great emphasis has alway been placed upon the cause-effect relation as fundamental for the maintenance of the *continuum* of a system. As the connection between the invariant antecedent and its consequent has proved empirically true, the axiom *continuity through determinism* has acquired a reassuring self-evident validity.

It is easily verifiable, however, that so far this relation has had to come to terms with such concepts as 'experience' and 'time' and as 'experience of time' as neither culture nor society are able to change unless these concepts also change.

It is worth noting that in Greek-Roman philosophy time was represented as circular and continuous and its continuity was determined by its measurability and divisibility into 'instants'. In some way antithetical to this, the Christian experience of time developed along a line proceeding from the Genesis to the Apocalypse according to a succession of such fixed points as 'before' and 'afterwards'. Modernity has conceived time as a secularisation of the linear irreversible Christian conception, depriving it of all idea of an end and emptying it of all meaning except that of the time-process itself.

Irreversibility in time extends the cause-effect relation in a new statement i.e. continuity in action causes continuity in variation. But as axioms do often remove non functional hypotheses, such rather obvious but latent phenomena as the universal dynamism of forms have often been neglected.

In fact the erosion of time on geological as well as on human and cultural 'forms' causes crises in the *continuum* in so far as it modifies the intrinsic quality of their structures. Any conflict and change in the structural quality of forms substantially modifies the cause-effect assumption and focuses attention on instability and discontinuity. On this basis a morphology of conflicts emerges and with it, a general Catastrophe Theory which states that any perturbation in a system induces the suspension of that system and the formation of a new one.

No doubt the dialectics of catastrophe founded on transformation has had a great metaphorical charge on the semiotic science. Émile Benveniste, for example, shows his rejection of linguistic determinism when he declares that le langage [. . .] n'est pas ni du continu ni de l'identique, mais bien au contraire du discontinu et du dissemblable.[8]

Language is, in the words of Benveniste, the medium apt to modify the quality of variations and therefore able to master the consequent, radical transformation of any logical co-ordinate. Language is the discontinuous *par excellence*, language is the vehicle of catastrophe.

René Thom's catastrophe theory, expressed by the author in his *Stabilité structurelle et Morphogenese* in 1972,[9] already implies metaphorical usage of the strictly scientific laws. In fact, in his *Logos phenix* he states that the fundamental syntactical mechanisms of a language are but the abstract copies of such biological conflictual functions in natural as predatism and sexual intercourse:

Les mécanisms syntaxiques les plus fondamentaux sont des copies simulatrices (définies sur un espace abstrait) des grandes fonctions regulatrices de la biologie (predation, rapport sexuel).[10]

This statement, explicitly based on the Heraclitean conception of a universal conflict by which and through which all things are generated, would probably be held by Samuel Beckett as a 'structural and dramatic convenience'[11] or 'inconvenience'[12] to which no 'truth value'[13] must be attached, although he himself has in some way theorised about catastrophies, probably unaware, long before the 1970s, when he deprived the Absurd of that theoretical universality which combines it—in the words of Theodor Adorno—'with the Western *pathos* of durability' (Preface to *Molloy, Malone meurt, L'Innommable*, 1958).

Beckett rejects existentialist conformism and lays his investigation within the hiatus, between before and afterward, that is, in the breach where congruity and coherence of sign and discourse become fortuitous; where semiotic entropy guarantees variety of narration but not its consistency; where semantic redundancy does not assure reliability. In Beckett's theatre catastrophe is both a *conflictual game* of simulation and a *formal structure* which investigates the relation between the phenomenic manifestation and its underlying system; i.e. its 'subworld' where no classification is allowed, no explicitation required ('the craze for explicitation') and whose phenomenon—the performance—is but the fight of nothingness for historical dimension.

On such an incongruous but inclusive stage, Beckett's forms wait, act, play; pseudo-humanity is excluded from any 'extensive' continuity but rather is included into 'intensive' dramatic verticality.

The surreal immobility of *Waiting for Godot*, already distils the crisis of the *continuum* by which Beckett's theatre seems profoundly affected. In it the word-gesture relation emerges as a conflict, substantially menaced as it is by the frequent shifts, indeed by the fragmentation of the sources of the dramatic message. Gesture gradually becomes detached from the dialogue to the point of producing meaning autonomously or in relation to a more and more inessential word. *L'ecart*, the gap between utterance, 'Let's go', and gesture '(they do not move)'[14] is the catastrophe the spectators are left with.

In *Act without Words I*, the performance crudely discloses a dumb ritual wholly played on the vertical exchange 'from flies' 'on stage', 'from stage' 'in flies'[15]. And yet the dialogue dwells upon the offering and acceptance of the objects which are in a necessary relation to the man's survival needs. When the objects are pulled up, they disappear together with the desire itself which had borne them. Immobility is again the 'ostensive' stage orientation through which the man addresses an audience now witness of the newly codified relation stimulus-non response.

In *Play* the conflictual pattern is drawn by a 'paradigmatic' ray of incidence—the spotlight—interfering with the horizontal order of the three urns ('touching one another three identical gray urns')[16]. An order which mimes the logical, syntagmatic course of the narration, the irreversible word chain which the spotlight abruptly interrupts and upsets, so that before acquiring completed meaning, narration is sharply suspended. The 'abrasions' on the signifying chain witnesses an induced aphasia which is intensely desired as appeasement in non-being.

With *Catastrophe* (1982), the last phase of the Aristotelian paradigm of tragedy is staged; in fact the rehearsal of the last scene of an anonymous 'pièce' is to be performed.

The metatheatrical device becomes apparent and explicit; the transparency of the signifying process is staged both as means and as object of the performance itself. The dramatic space is bare indeed reduced to a bare point defined by the position of P, the archetype of all protagonists, whereas the audience space is usurped by Director 'sitting downstairs audience left'.

Being a rehearsal the performance seems to be acted *in absentia* but the spectators are included in the dramatic exchange as the main interlocutors of this sort of 'aside' and themselves among the actors. Ages and physiques of the *dramatis personae* are 'unimportant', on the contrary their positions and costumes are focused as substantially determining their dramatic roles:

Luke in charge of lighting, offstage.
D in an armchair downstairs /. . ./ Fur coat. Fur toque to match.
A standing beside him. White overall. Bare head. Pencil on ear.
P midstage on a black block 18 inches high. Black wide-brimmed hat. Black dressing gown to ankles. Barefoot. Head bowed. Hands in pockets.[17]

Each of them writes his own code and performs it in three different theatrical *loci*: onstage, offstage, the pit. Three different theatrical codes ask to be decoded simultaneously but the organic wholeness of the dramatic message is fragmented for ever and its totality parodied. The two extremes P and D mark the limits of this sort of vertical space which cuts across the horizontal continuum of the conventional stage. The interaction between P and D is insisted on, hysterical and is reduced to the invisible geometrical trajectory drawn by Assistant stepping up and down the stage.

Verticality helps veil the face but unveils the feet through an alternate play 'to have him all black' but also a kind of extorted birth-death. P's blackness is not provoked by Luke who has just set the light, but rather it is organic blackness, the blackness inside a cocoon or a womb nourishing a skull and two crippled hands.

A few touches—to which P 'submits, inert' or imperceptibly 'shivering'—transforms the black gown into the white shroud of nudity. Moult or birth: no need to make it explicit; no gag which would interrupt the action and delay the dénouement and, what is more, which would induce a new code and codify the incongruous.

D and A contemplate P. Long pause
A: *Finally* Like the look of him?
D: So so. *Pause* Why the plinth?
A/ To let the stalls see the feet.
Pause
D/ Why the hat?
A: To help hide the face.
Pause
D: Why the gown?
A: To have him all black.[18]

Once the machinery has been displayed and the fictitious unveiled, the theatrical labour becomes a substitution for conventional metaphysical and 'historical' links between soul and body, cause and effect, God and creatures, Director and Protagonist, Master and Slave.

But when Director exits 'not to appear again', 'A subsides in the armchair, springs to her feet no sooner seated, takes out rag, wipes vigorously back seat of chair, discards rag, sits again'. A plays her own gag and metaphorically provides the piece with the referent code of substitution and simulation. In fact each dramatis persona is the invariant fictitious mirror of various parodic doubles, i.e. the director, assistant and light technician of each performance; instead P's role is unique despite the multiplicity of interpretations. Such an effect of simulation enlivens the play with phantasmata which are signs raised to the nth power almost to the point of hiding the generative image, the Ur-image on the stage.

Luke has not appeared on the stage so far and will not till the end. He is the hidden executor to whom Assistant transmits Director's orders in technical terms. Light is no longer the metaphysical spotlight acting in *Play* almost as *causa sui*. Luke's light contributes to prepare the final scene, the catastrophe of the anonymous piece being acted on stage. Meantime A insists on letting P 'raise his head . . . show his face an instant . . .' but D: 'for God's sake! Raise his head? Where do you think we are? In Patagonia? Raise his head? For God's sake. Good. *There is our catastrophe.*'[19] There is the Christ by Mantegha. No need to make it explicit. The paradigm is over.

In the words of Aristotle: 'catastrophe is an action bringing ruin and pain on stage, where corpses are seen and wounds and other similar sufferings performed'.[20]

Theatre has extinguished its *pathos* and has extinguished itself in *pathos*. But unexpectedly 'P raises his head, fixes his audience. The applause falters. Dies'.[21] P had eluded instructions, the metaphor has escaped the metaphorizer, the phenomenon has denied and betrayed its underlying structure. *Mourir de ne pas pouvoir mourir* (Dying of not being able to die) is the contemporary catastrophe.

What Where, first published in 1984, opens on the deceptive uniformity of the *dramatis personae*: 'Bam, Bem, Bim, Bom'. One name though with its vowel alterations; one form sundered into four.

Same long grey gown
Same long grey hair.[22]

One figure of speech, analogy, which creates deceptive references and indeed cancels identity. The dimly lit, rectangular scene is the playing area of both a play and a ritual.

The uttered text opens on a lie as well. 'We are the last five' but V is Bam's voice as the attempt to make voices and *dramatis personae* coincide, gives incongruous results. The journey through the ordered succession of seasons 'It is Spring', 'It is Summer', 'It is Autumn', 'It is Winter', leads to the centre of a temporal labyrinth whose map has been drawn in sufferings.

The dramatic exchange assimilates voice to light. At each suspension of light ('I switch on', 'I start again') the whole play is entirely re-acted and the expectation of sense, so exasperatedly aroused through sharp interruptions, is frustrated by the performance of an act without words, first, and by its re-play with words, successively, though no evolution in meaning occurs. These will display, rather, the mere acts of coding and re-coding, a kind of staged translation charged with remote echoes:

V: We are the last five.
In the present as we were still.
It is spring.
Time passes.
First without words.[23]

I am alone.
It is spring.
Time passes.
Now with words.[24]

The dialogue which doubles the pantomime seems to refer to a refusal to confess an unnamable crime on the part of a 'he' who, because of that 'was given the works', 'wept', 'screamed', 'begged for mercy'. When re-acted the victimizer has become the victim, Bom is beaten by Bim, Bim is beaten by Bom, Bem is beaten by Bam and so in an obsessive chain of cruelty. The scientific law of the universal conflict is deprived of all cultural implications and denotes itself as mere predatism.

No doubt then the riddle to which each *dramatis persona* is subjected, playful in rhythm and cruel in subject, is akin to certain nursery rhymes which through centuries and civilizations, have kept alive the collective memory of ancient sacrificial rites or to which the function of liberating the collective unconscious has been attached.

In *What Where* the obsessive repetition is marked by slightly varied lessemes, which adding nothing to sense are but illusory traces leading to the core of the final enigma. The linguistic involution, in fact, records both the horror of ineluctability and the gradual emptying of all identity and situational references. So sense fades out and while denying itself to the audience, transfers to it the anxiety of the solution.

V: Good
It is winter.
Time passes.
In the end I appear.
Reappear.

Bam enters at W, halts at 3 head bowed

V: Good.
I am alone.
In the present as were I still.
It is winter.
Without journey.
Time passes.
That is all.
Make sense who may.
I switch off.[25]

Language is the vehicle of the perturbation occurring between the self and the Otherness whose inert consciousness is now called to the anxiety of decoding. Gradually the 'enigmatic' situation assumes the form of a ritual trial in so far as the positions of the proposer ('In the end I appear') and the solver become the seat of a conflict which must be overcome by the efforts of the latter. Thus the trial acquires initiatic quality and the enigma becomes the passage through which the solver undergoes a change in status.

'Make sense who may' is therefore a challenge both to 'claritas' in meaning and to time as a *continuum*, a trial belonging to those rites of passage which might be able to transform the archetypes of contemporaneity. Otherness, both the object and the medium of the enigma proposed, discloses itself as solver *in nuce* of metaphorical obscurity and its attempts of solution are but the means through which it risks its own historical presence.

CATASTROPHE AND DRAMATIC SETTING

HERSH ZEIFMAN

Roughly midway through the second act of *En attendant Godot*, Estragon, weary of Vladimir's games and wanting desperately to leave, rushes offstage first into one wing and then the other, only to return both times terrified at the approach of unknown people blocking any possible escape; as Vladimir comments, 'Nous sommes cernés!' Gogo's two journeys offstage have taken him, in each instance, to the edge of the slope—'jusqu'au bord de la pente'—causing Didi to observe: 'En effet, nous sommes sur un plateau. Aucun doute, nous sommes servis sur un plateau.'[1] I am citing the original French text here because Didi's observation does not appear in Beckett's English translation of *Godot*—perhaps not surprisingly, since the phrase 'servis sur un plateau' is a multilayered pun, working on at least three different levels. In the immediate context, Didi is simply stating that they happen to be caught on a plain. But 'plateau' also means 'tray' and 'stage'; thus the tramps are in addition both 'served up on a platter' and 'trapped on the stage'. Literally and figuratively, then, they are presented as helpless victims waiting to be destroyed.

The above passage is obviously interesting from a linguistic point of view, attesting to Beckett's masterful way with words and to the importance of verbal subtext in his drama. But it also provides a significant clue to the nature of setting in Beckett's early plays. For the three connotations of 'servis sur un plateau' correspond to three distinct senses in which one can speak of Beckett's dramatic setting. There is, first of all, setting as *landscape* ('caught on a plain'): the plays are situated in some kind of geographical or domestic terrain, however vague or unspecified, a literal setting that exists on the stage. On a second level there is setting as *soulscape* ('served up on a platter'): what we are dealing with here might be termed inner landscape, the figurative setting that exists within a character's mind. And finally there is setting as *theatrical space* ('caught on a stage'): wherever else we may be in Beckett's drama—whether an actual place or the inside of a character's head—we are always, Beckett is at pains to remind us, in a theatre watching a play.

This trilevel setting is a distinctive feature not only of *Godot*, but of other early Beckett plays. The setting of *Endgame*, for example, consists, in one sense, of the *Bare interior. Grey light* we see literally before us—a room with a door, two small curtained windows high up, a picture with its face to the wall, and two ashbins covered with an old sheet.[2] In another sense, however, the setting may be said to consist of the inside of the characters' heads. For the room resembles a skull—bare, grey, the two small windows reminiscent of eye sockets, the walls hollow: 'Do you hear? (*[Hamm] strikes the wall with his knuckles.*) Do you hear? Hollow bricks! (*He strikes again.*) All that's hollow!' (p. 26). The symbolism of a skull-like set suggests Christ's crucifixion at Golgotha, 'a place of a skull',[3] and thus evokes the intense suffering of the play's characters. But it also implies that the play's setting is primarily an internal one—not so much a wall, say, as the figurative writing on the wall. 'And what do you see on your wall?', Hamm sardonically asks Clov at one point in the play. 'Mene, mene?' (p. 12). It is what the characters 'see' in their mind's eye that truly creates the bleak and desolate world of *Endgame*, a kingdom that has been numbered and finished[4]—like the vision of the mad painter Hamm recalls visiting in the asylum, a vision which the four pawn of *Endgame*, the four 'speck[s] in the void' (p. 36), share:

> I'd take him by the hand and drag him to the window. Look! There! All that rising corn! And there! Look! The sails of the herring fleet! All the loveliness! (*Pause.*) He'd snatch away his hand and go back into his corner. Appalled. All he had seen was ashes. (p. 44)

The characters' room with a view, then, turns out in fact to be a skull, its view directed inward rather than outward. But the bones of this skull are also the boards of the stage, on which the characters perform specifically theatrical roles. 'Me [. . .] to play' (p. 2) begins Hamm, that ham actor obsessed with being literally centre stage (pp. 25-27, 76). In this 'farce' (p. 32) of an endgame, the only thing that keeps them there, as Hamm wickedly points out, is '[t]he dialogue' (p. 58). 'Did anyone ever have pity on me?' questions Hamm rhetorically. Clov responds: 'Is it me you're referring to?' 'An aside, ape!', retorts Hamm. 'Did you never hear an aside before? (*Pause.*) I'm warming up for my last soliloquy' (pp. 77-78). And when Clov thinks he has spied something outside through his telescope—the same telescope he had earlier turned on the audience, claiming, 'I see . . . a multitude . . . in transports . . . of joy (*Pause.*) That's what I call a magnifier'. (p. 29)—Hamm's response is 'Not an underplot, I trust' (p. 78). 'Let's stop playing!' implores Clov near the end of the play, to which Hamm replies 'Never!' (p. 77). And Hamm is prophetically right, for their torment never ceases; at best there will be a brief pause, a momentary stasis, until the next evening's performance of *Endgame* begins the cycle all over again. In this impoverished world that is a stage, all the men and women of *Endgame* are merely players, with their painful entrances and false exits—'This is what we call making an exit' (p. 81), Clov comments as he tries repeatedly to leave the stage—self-conscously strutting and fretting their hours to the last syllable of recorded time.

As Beckett continued to write plays in the 1960s and '70s, as he continued to chip away at all the superfluities of dramatic form, his plays became shorter, bleaker, more intensely focused—a movement towards minimalism, towards what Edith Kern, in an admirable phrase, once termed 'drama stripped for inaction'.[5] And the trilevel setting of Beckett's earlier plays underwent a similar transformation. In late plays like *Not I* and *Footfalls*, for example, the first level of setting, the level of landscape, essentially disappears. The landscape of *Godot* may be minimal and vague—a road, a tree, a mound—but it is something to hold on to; we may not know exactly where we are, but we know we are somewhere in the world. *Not I*, on the other hand, seems to be set literally nowhere (at any rate, nowhere in *this* world): there are no visual clues to any external setting whatsoever. The play seems instead to be set in Mouth's head—the maddened stream-of-consciousness of a mind refusing to relinquish the third person, refusing to acknowledge that the situation she is narrating is in fact her own. Or it may be said to be set simply in theatrical space: a disembodied Mouth is magically suspended eight feet in the air, trapped by the mechanics of theatre as surely as by the convolutions of her mind, spewing forth a feverish torrent of words that bores painfully into our skulls, lit by an immobile spotlight that ultimately appears to change shape and position in front of our eyes. The audience is being, in effect, viscerally assaulted, experiencing in the theatre what Mouth is experiencing. And the presence of the Auditor, in both senses of his name, reinforces this double setting of mind and theatre. On the one hand, he can be seen as a projection of Mouth's own psyche, the visual symbol of an internal correcting process that attempts to audit, attempts to examine and assess the validity of, her account(s); on the other hand, he becomes a surrogate for us as audience, the auditor as listener intent on Mouth's narration.[6]

In *Footfalls*, the setting is similarly double-level. May's endless pacing up and down that narrow strip at the front of the stage, nine steps and then wheel about, is more a mental than a physical journey, as V, the offstage voice of her mother, clearly implies:

V: Will you never have done? (*Pause.*) Will you never have done . . . revolving it all?
M: (*halting*): It?
V: It all. (*Pause.*) In your poor mind.[7]

Nor is V herself necessarily a literal, external presence. In the first British publication of *Footfalls*, based with some exceptions for reasons unknown, on Beckett's penultimate typescript, V's monologue in the play's second section begins: 'I walk here now. (*Pause.*) Rather I come and stand. (*Pause.*) At nightfall. (*Pause.*) My voice is in her mind.'[8] Although Beckett's final version eliminated all explicit references to V's emanating from within May, the feeling nevertheless remains strong that *Footfalls* is set in May's mind. May thus *subsumes* her mother, as the name May subsumes ma. And the progress of her mental journey is measured more in the pacing of her voiced thoughts than in the pacing of her feet; the footfalls she is so desperate to hear are, in fact, internal ones. As T. S. Eliot wrote in *Burnt Norton*: 'Footfalls echo in the memory . . . / My words echo / Thus, in your mind.'[9]

A second way of describing the setting of *Footfalls* is to place it specifically in theatrical space. For at the centre of the play is the image of May's constant pacing, the sound of her '*clearly audible rhythmic tread*' (p. 42). Where is she, it may be asked. The question is V's, but it is our question too. V's answer is that May is 'in the old home' (p. 45), walking back and forth along a once carpeted but now bare floor, occasionally stopping and standing still with her face to the wall. But the audience does not see that old home; May's pacing is, for us, confined simply to a one-metre strip at the front of the stage. The boards she is pacing are the boards of the theatre, not the floorboards at home. And when she comes to rest and stares straight ahead, it is not at a wall but at us, the theatre audience. May—a character who has not quite been born, who only *may* exist, who wears, according to Beckett, 'the costume of a ghost'[10]—is present for us only in the theatre: a spectral apparition in a truncated four-act tragedy, in each act ever more faintly lit, ever more faintly there, finally disappearing without a trace—until, of course, the next haunting performance of *Footfalls*.

The setting of Beckett's late plays, then, becomes progressively shrunken, progressively internalised, leaving macrocosm behind for microcosm: the enclosed planes of a skull, the enclosed space of a stage. '"I am not of the big world, I am of the little world" was an old refrain of Murphy' wrote Beckett in his first published novel; [11] and that refrain is echoed again and again in his recent theatre. Except, many have argued, in *Catastrophe*. For the setting of *Catastrophe* seems to differ significantly from the setting of Beckett's other late plays. On the one hand, 'landscape' reappears: we seem to be in an actual, identifiable place that exists out there in the world. 'Soulscape', on the other hand, disappears: *Catastrophe* seems to be dramatised externally, from the outside looking in, rather than the other way around—we are no longer inside someone's head. This apparent shift in setting accompanies what has been seen as a corresponding shift in theme; almost every journalist and critic who has written on the play has categorised it as a radically new departure for Beckett's theatre: a play overtly about politics.[12] Clearly there are grounds for such critical assessment. Written in French at the invitation of A. I. D. A. (Association Internationale de Défense des Artistes) and dedicated to the Czech dissident writer Vaclǻv Havel, *Catastrophe* was first performed in July 1982 at the Avignon Festival as part of an evening of plays honouring Havel, who was at the time in prison. Even without this knowledge of the specific circumstances surrounding the play's inception, however, a critic might easily be tempted to interpret the central action of *Catastrophe* in political terms: the play certainly appears to be about political torture and the heartless cruelty of the state's supression of human rights.

Without at all questioning Beckett's genuine concern with the issue of political and artistic repression, and without impugning the response of those inclined to interpret the play as a political parable, I should like nevertheless to suggest that the critical consensus concerning *Catastrophe*, in terms of both its setting and its theme, may be misleading. Let us begin with the apparent return in the play of what I have been calling 'landscape'. Ironically enough, this external setting of *Catastrophe* turns out to be a theatre, in which the Director and his Assistant are rehearsing the '*[f]inal touches to the last scene*'[13] of some kind of dramatic presentation. But are we really in an actual theatre as such? After the Director has completed those final touches, arranging to his satisfaction the Protagonist's clothes, makeup and posture, he states 'I'll go and see how it looks from the house. *Exit* D, *not to appear again*' (p. 32). But although this is our last sight of D, it is not our last awareness of his presence, for the very next line in the text is D's offstage voice irritably noting 'can't see the toes. [. . .] I'm sitting in the front row of the stalls and can't see the toes' (p. 32). Where is D speaking from? He claims to be in the 'house', specifically 'in the front row of the stalls', but manifestly not in *our* theatre: his voice instead floats out of the darkness in some theatrical limbo. At rehearsals for the New York premiere of *Catastrophe* in 1983, director Alan Schneider suggested that, at this moment, 'the audience must feel disoriented. The voice rises within what might be a vast theatre space, or some echoing void . . .'[14] Rosette Lamont has rightly described audience reaction at this point as a feeling of 'eeriness':[15] we have assumed that the setting of *Catastrophe* is an actual theatre—presumably the theatre in which we ourselves are sitting—and yet D's actions shatter that illusion. As opposed to the 'landscape' of a literal theatre, then, the setting of *Catastrophe* is more properly theatrical space: the '*[b]are stage*' (p. 25) on which all of Beckett's plays are fundamentally set. And, as always, this concept of setting as theatrical space in Beckett's drama is a signpost of metatheatre: on one level, Beckett is constantly writing plays about writing plays, about performing plays.

In that respect, *Catastrophe* is no exception. P, the Protagonist of both the frame play in *Catastrophe* and the play-within-the-play, is in many ways a pitiful creature: his heartbreaking appearance and the dehumanized way in which he is treated have led many critics to see in him the inmate of a concentration camp or gulag. But he is also the image of most of the characters in Beckett's last plays: a figure in pain, physically degenerating, dressed in black over ash, the colours of death. And in this inner play so powerfully evocative of Beckett's late drama, P is not merely the leading character, but, ultimately, the representation of *the play itself*. He is the raw material, the clay, which the Director is so desperate to shape and to mould. If P is thus seen as embodying the essence of a Beckettian text, then the central action of *Catastrophe* is not primarily about political repression, but about another form of 'tyranny', the tyranny of theatrical production. The Director—so slimy that his Assistant instinctively wipes the chair he has been occupying before sitting in it herself (p. 32)—is a close relation of that other major tyrant in Beckett's drama: Pozzo. Both are obsessed with power, with chronometers and a specific timetable to be met, with the illusion of control. 'Higher', D barks at his underling, overseeing her manipulation of P. 'A touch more. [. . .] Stop!' (p. 31), echoing Pozzo's commands to *his* underling, Lucky: 'Back! [. . .] Further! [. . .] Stop!'[16] But D's tyranny is more particularized than Pozzo's. Deliberately rejecting 'this craze for explicitation!',[17] relying on the aid of his Assistant and a lighting technician called Luke, D confidently sets out to shape a text for performance: manipulating it, refining it, 'taming' it into submission. The process is apparently successful: godlike, D gazes proudly at his final creation and sees that it is 'Good', exulting 'There's our catastrophe' (p. 35). In the New York production, Donald Davis as D pronounced 'catastrophe' as a three-syllable word with the accent on the first syllable and the final 'e' silent, thus echoing the original French but, more important, emphasizing its Greek etymology and primary meaning: 'The change which produces the final event of a dramatic piece; the dénouement.'[18] *Catastrophe*, then, is not a play focusing primarily on politics which uses theatre as a kind of metaphor, but rather the reverse: it is a play focusing primarily on theatre from which a political interpretation may be inferred. P is indeed a prisoner, but his confinement is specifically within the straitjacket of theatrical production: like Didi and Gogo, like the text of a Beckett play itself, he is 'trapped on the stage'.

Or is he? Despite D's boast that the 'catastrophe' is '[i]n the bag' (p. 35), can a Beckett text ever be 'captured' in quite this way? D thinks he is in total control, dazzling us with the truth of his stage picture of P: the gospel lit according to Luke. But this Luke is no saint and this 'gospel' not the bearer of good news for D; Luke's light, the light embodied in his very name, is deceptive—as deceptive as is the other kind of 'light' which D thrice summons for his cigar but which repeatedly goes out on him (pp. 27, 29, 31). The light provided by Luke does not go out, but something equally startling occurs. In the midst of D's apparent success ('Terrific! He'll have them on their feet. I can hear it from here. *Pause. Distant storm of applause*'), P '*raises his head, fixes the audience. The applause falters, dies. Long pause*' (p. 36). P's look stops the play dead, unsettling the audience—both the anticipated audience of D's reverie and the actual audience watching in the theatre. For a long, unbearable poignant moment of time, P fixes us with his eyes, the '[s]eat of all',[19] the windows of the soul; and through those eyes we enter P's head—that 'cranium' (p. 30), that 'skull' of '[a]sh' (p. 27). The play's setting has suddenly shifted, at the very last moment, into P's mind—a shift that represents P's Pyrrhic victory. For D is ultimately proved wrong: *here* is the real 'catastrophe' of the play, the true dénouement. And it lies entirely outside D's control. However much he is prodded and manipulated, there is something in P—something in the text of a Beckett play—that resists being programmed or controlled, something with a 'mind' of its own: a kind of integrity, perhaps, a stubborn intransigence that can never fully be captured or tamed by performance.

Or perhaps it is not so much integrity as simply an elusive core—not so much a gesture of defiance on P's part as an acknowledgement of impossibility. In the spring of 1983, Beckett explained to Rosette Lamont how he had started to write for the stage: 'When I was working on *Watt*', Beckett commented, 'I felt the need to create for a smaller space, one in which I had some control of where people stood or moved, above all of a certain light. I wrote *Waiting for Godot*'.[20] Beckett's control of dramatic text as a playwright, and of theatrical performance as a director, is breathtaking. And yet, that notion of total mastery is ultimately illusory, for there remains an essential 'control' always beyond Beckett's power; the quest to 'eff the ineffable',[21] whether as playwright or director, is by definition doomed to failure. In *Catastrophe*, both D and P are, in their different ways, images of that failure. When at the end of the play P suddenly lifts his head and fixes us with his look, we thus have a 'catastrophe' in two senses of the word. P's gesture provides the play's genuine catastrophe as opposed to D's manufactured one: the true dénouement is P's dogged refusal to be shaped and manipulated, to be mastered—the text rebelling against being captured by theatrical performance. But that same rebellion is also a catastrophe in the second, more usual sense of the word: the sign of a sudden, great disaster. For it symbolizes once more the futility of Beckett's quest, his admission that 'to be an artist is to fail, as no other dare fail, that failure is his world and the shrink from it desertion, art and craft, good housekeeping, living'.[22]

Despite its political overtones, then, *Catastrophe* does not really represent a radical departure for Beckett. Set like his other late plays in both theatrical space and, for one searing moment, the inside of the protagonist's head, it deals like them with the inner workings of both a mind and a play. Like the fifth-act Hamlet tottering on the edge of a grave, Beckett is as usual playing with a skull: the inside of a head, the skeleton of a theatrical work. In that fixed stare with which P immobilizes us lies Beckett's eternal 'catastrophe': 'All of old. Nothing else ever. Ever tried. Ever failed. No matter. Try again. Fail again. Fail better'[23]—the mystery and elusiveness of his theatrical art.

A POLITICAL PERSPECTIVE ON *CATASTROPHE*

ROBERT SANDARG

Catastrophe, the most tangible and powerful of Beckett's later dramas, is a compassionate testimony to the cause of human rights; it marks an undeniable political engagement on Beckett's part and may lead us to reevaluate his entire canon from the perspective of social consciousness.

Politics, commitment and society . . . a blasphemy of Beckett? Not in the least. Samuel Beckett is a man who has lived through the turmoil of modern history. He writes not from beyond space and time but from the cultural context of twentieth-century Europe. To consider Beckett politically innocent would be naive, given his work in the French Resistance and his efforts on behalf of the Polish refugee Adam Tarn and the Spanish playwright Fernando Arrabal. When Tarn, whose drama journal included news of Western theatrical developments, was forced by the Communist government to leave Warsaw in 1964, Beckett helped him relocate in Canada. During the autumn of 1968, Beckett made his first direct political statement since World War II when he joined a number of prominent French intellectuals who signed letters of protest to the Spanish authorities in Madrid decrying the imprisonment of Arrabal for supposed obscenity and treason against the Franco regime.

Beckett writes on many levels—the ethical, the religious, the symbolic; and although historico-political considerations are not paramount to his oeuvre, they do occupy a significant place. In *Endgame*, Nell's allusion to Sedan conjures up the defeat of Napoleon III in 1871, while the poem 'Saint-Lô' treats the aftermath of a battle in this century. The glazier in *Eleuthéria* berates Victor as 'the poor young man, the heroic young man, shot by Franco, shot by Stalin', while Hairy Quin compares Walter Draffin to a kind of rubber Stalin in *More Pricks than Kicks*. The interrogators Bim and Bom in *What Where*, like those sadistic madhouse attendants Bim and Bom Clinch from *Murphy*, evoke the Soviet clowns Bim and Bom and the Stalinist era.

S. E. Gontarski notes that 'both *Endgame* and *Happy Days* are permeated with the suggestion of nuclear devastation. . . . In the early mss of *Happy Days*, Willie, called simply B, reads from his yellowed newspaper: "Rocket strikes Pomona, seven hundred thousand missing" . . . "Rocket strikes Man, one female lavatory attendant spared" . . . "Aberrant rocket strikes Erin, eighty-three priests survive."'[1] Director Walter Asmus reports that Beckett wanted actors in the televised German version of *What Where* to appear not bareheaded, in accordance with stage directions, but to wear fezzes. He intended this revision as nothing less than an allusion to contemporaneous political unrest in Turkey. Ultimately, but only for practical, technical reasons, plastic caps were substituted.

In fact, *Rough for Radio II*, written during the early 1960s, *Catastrophe* plus *What Where* (1983) may be considered a triptych inspired by modern political circumstances. *Rough* is a very rough interrogation session during which Fox is physically and psychically destroyed by the effects of blinders, earplugs, gag and blows of the bull's pizzle. *Catastrophe* might be the aftermath of this torture seance, with the victim on state display, while *What Where* is a full-scale purge sparked by vicious but abortive inquisitions.

BAM: You gave him the works?
BOM: Yes.
BAM: And he didn't say it?
BOM: No.
BAM: He wept?
BOM: Yes.
BAM: Screamed?
BOM: Yes.
BAM: Begged for mercy?
BOM: Yes.
BAM: But didn't say it?
BOM: No.
BAM: Then why stop?
BOM: He passed out.[2]

Since no confessions are reported the failed interrogators Bim, Bom and Bem are purged by the disbelieving Bam who tells each in turn, 'It's a lie. He said it to you. Confess he said it to you. You'll be given the works until you confess'.[3] Moreover, the radio in the title *Rough for Radio II*, like the onstage presence in *Catastrophe*, is as recognizable a propaganda device as Genet's balcony, upon which dictators raved. The devilishly indeterminate megaphone in *What Where* suggests the limitless powers of contemporary and future diffusion, for it broadcasts the voice of Bam who dominates 'through the seasons'.

Understandably, critics have proffered clearly political interpretations for several other works by Beckett, calling *Waiting For Godot* an allegory of French resistance to the Germans, Irish resistance to the English or Beckett's escape to Roussillon. For Marxists who see *Waiting For Godot* in terms of class struggle, Godot's appearance would mark the advent of the classless society. Indeed, when Brecht read *Godot* in 1953 he envisioned mounting it with Pozzo as landowner, Estragon a prole, Vladimir an intellectual and Lucky a cop or a jackass. Furthermore, Brecht planned to spice the performance with documentary background films of Red China.[4]

In the early 1960s Alan Schneider participated in a symposium during which playwright John Arden attacked Beckett for remaining aloof and not writing plays about the Algerian crisis. Responding irately, Schneider affirmed that all Beckett's plays were about Algeria in the metaphorical sense.[5] Vivian Mercier put the matter of political derivation another way. 'It is a measure of Beckett's art that he invokes this tradition stealthily rather than blatantly.'[6]

Hugh Kenner wrote frostily:

> When *Play* was first offered a critic was heard to object that Beckett had at last surrendered all contact with reality. That was only a generation since . . . the Gestapo had led prisoners through their stories, over and over, under the lights. . . . It even seems feasible to link the Gestapo itself to the iron discipline of orderly prose, which prescribes for you, sentence by sentence, what you are at liberty (liberty!) to say.[7]

Regarding *Catastrophe*, Schneider reaffirmed Beckett's political consciousness even more concretely. 'He's always had that', Schneider maintained. 'He just didn't write plays with obviously political subjects. . . . He's not a man removed from reality.'[8]

Thus, when AIDA solicited works for a Nuit Václav Havel, Beckett was among the first to respond. Havel had been active in the Prague theatrical world since the late 1950s when he became assistant director of Alfred Radok's multidimensional Lanterna Magica theatre, then worked in the avant-garde Ná Zabradlí theatre. Havel's international debut came in 1963 with *Zahradní Slavnost* (*Garden Party*), a comedy bordering on theatre of the absurd which exposed socialism as phraseological gibberish masking despotism. In 1965 he attacked the communist bureaucracy in *Vyrozumění* (*Notification*).

Following the Soviet invasion of 1968 Havel's works were banned, but this playwright with the obligation to express and the words with which to express continued in the *samizdat* or, to use the Czech term, *edice petlice* tradition, his play being performed clandestinely for minuscule audiences behind locked apartment doors, then smuggled out of Czechoslovakia to be printed in France, Sweden, West Germany and Canada. In 1969 Havel received the State Prize of the Austrian Republic. Pressured to emigrate, he refused and instead became a founding member of the Czech human rights organization Chapter 77. Havel remained under house arrest from 1977 until 1979, when he was sentenced to four and one half years imprisonment for subversion. He was incarcerated when Beckett wrote *Catastrophe* and was transferred to a hospital in 1983.

Let us now turn to *Catastrophe*, which is really many catastrophes—a play 'for Václav Havel.'

We find ourselves spectators at the metatheatrical rehearsal of a final, tragic scene—a catastrophe in the sense of dénouement. An overbearing Director and his female Assistant nearly strip the Protagonist, a figure cowering atop an eighteen inch block, and mould him like clay into a statue of silent suffering, to a final storm of recorded applause.

The stage setting is sparse, black and white, but the modern costuming highly evocative. The Director is a commissar in ostentatious fur coat and toque. Dressed for a chilling Prague winter, he is on his way to a caucus. His Assistant is a pencil-pushing bureaucrat ceaselessly taking notes, an apparatchik working over this refusenik of a Protagonist who is clad in gray pyjamas beneath a black hat and dressing gown.

Beckett's works have always included a carceral dimension—Pentonville Prison in *Murphy*, the 'enormous prison, like a hundred thousand cathedrals' in *The Unnamable*, the Mountjoy Prison where McCabe awaited execution in *More Pricks Than Kicks*. There exists also in Beckett a constant sense of surveillance, as expressed by Vladimir, Winnie and Molloy, plus a striking abundance of mental hospitals both factual and fictional. The Bethlehem Royal Hospital, Magdalen Mental Mercyseat, the mansions (or madhouse cells) in *Watt*, Saint John of Gods and the Portrane Lunatic Asylum acquire a timely and disturbing significance these days when political prisoners are condemned not only to Gulags but *cured* in hospitals and madhouses where dressing gown and pyjamas form the standard uniform.

In this regard, Beckett's early fiction was sadly prophetic. 'We shall think and act for you from now forward', announces the asylum staff in *Malone Dies*, while in the tale 'Fingal' the regimented lunatics 'seem very sane'. As for the recalcritrant, prisoners of conscience, hunger strikers? 'I sit on them that will not eat, jacking their jaws apart with the gag, spurning their tongues aside with the spatula, till the last tundish of drench is absorbed', growled Ticklepenny in *Murphy*.[9]

Returning to the production, here stands the Protagonist. 'Our catastrophe. In the bag', sneers the Director. This would-be fomentor of events that overturn the order, the system of things (the etymology of catastrophe being 'to turn upside down') appears beaten. Shivering, head hanging, chest exposed, trousers rolled, voiceless among the voices, he resembles a prisoner prepared for an official visit or a propaganda warning for *all* to see in *all* his agony. 'I can't see the toes', shouts the Director irritably. 'I'm sitting in the front row of the stalls and I can't see the toes.'[10]

The Protagonist would seem a burnt out case and indeed, flame and ash form the basic symbology of this play. This connection is strikingly apparent in the French, given the actual juxtaposition of the words *cendre* and *feu*.

A Sa tenue de nuit.
M Couleur?
A Cendre.
M sort un cigare.
M Du feu.[11]

The Assistant lights the Director's cigar, which is as opulent as Mr. Endon's in *Murphy*, three separate times, while the Protagonist is reduced to ashes.

A: His night attire.
D: Colour?
A: Ash . . .

D: How's the skull?
A: Moulting. A few tufts.
D: Colour?
A: Ash.[12]

In *Godot*, the dead make a noise 'like feathers . . . like leaves . . . like ashes'. Moreover, the Director gives the order to make the Protagonist even more ashen. Whiten his cranium, whiten all his flesh, incinerate his spirit and his body if need be. Drive him beyond the decrepitude of Nagg and Nell in ash bins, to the deadened, ashen world of the mad engraver in *Endgame* or the final resting state of Murphy—ashes scattered among the spits and slops of a bar-room floor!

Catastrophe concludes with the Protagonist still speechless (he never utters a word) and trembling atop his plinth. But has he been defeated? Despite his pitiful state, it seems not; for in the midst of the canned applause in which one critic heard hoofbeats and the grinding wheels of approaching tumbrels, the Protagonist, according to Beckett's stage directions, 'raises his head and fixes the audience. The applause falters, dies'. The Protagonist is not staring at the public in abject supplication. Beckett told Mel Gussow that 'it was not his intention to have the character make an appeal. . . . He is a triumphant martyr rather than a sacrificial victim . . . and is meant to cow onlookers into submission through the intensity of his gaze and his stoicism'.[13]

The Protagonist's stoicism brings us to yet a third definition of catastrophe, found in *Malone Dies*. 'Catastrophe in the ancient sense . . . To be buried in lava and not turn a hair, it is then a man shows what stuff he is made of.'[14] Reduced to ashes beneath volcanic totalitarianism, the Protagonist endures. Perhaps he will rise Phoenix-like from his ashes and his silence (silence being the end *and* the beginning of all things) while the flame associated with the Director and his Assistant will splutter out with increasing frequency, then die. There is ash on the Director's cigar, too, and it is not 'firm and blue' like that on Moran's in *Molloy*.

We cannot assert that the Protagonist is definitely Václav Havel, any more than we could claim that Alfred Peron, to whom Beckett dedicated the French translation of *Murphy*, is the gull-eyed Murphy. One can go too far, to quote the Director, in 'this craze for explicitation. Every i dotted to death . . . For God's sake'. But if theatre and literature are to be 'vitally engaged with the living situation . . . they must countenance social and historical realities'.[15] And the real bedrock of *Catastrophe* lies in the imagery of a modern totalitarian state which dehumanizes its victims.

Beckett has always talked of tyrants—the Pozzos, Hamms and especially God, that old fornicator; but now the State has replaced the deity, and with an institutionalised terror apparatus that Gabriel Marcel called *les techniques d'avilissement*, has transformed its subjects into suspects filled with fear and unnamed guilt and infinitely malleable. The process of human degradation that occurs throughout Beckett's oeuvre—the stumbling that becomes rolling that becomes crawling—is accelerated by the ravages of the corporate state. It is little wonder that *Catastrophe* inspired the South African playwright Maishe Mapoyna's *Gangsters*, which deals with the illegal incarceration of Steve Biko.

Of course, *Catastrophe*, like all of Beckett's works, harbours a multiplicity of meanings. It is not a treatise, it is art—total theatre that goes far beyond a transcription of the surface, or facade, to hark back to Beckett's essay on Proust. The Protagonist may be the generalised artist manipulated by society or tortured by the agony of the creative process. After all, shorn of its dedication to Havel, *Catastrophe* was allowed to be played in Poland. By the same token, *Rough For Radio II* may concern a critic torturing an author. The Animator speaks of Sterne and Dante, 'old spectres from the days of book reviewing', and the twin which Fox carries monstrously within himself could be his book. Similarly, *What Where* which ends, 'That is all. Make sense who may. I switch off', might treat not of a purge but, according to Alan Schneider, 'the impossibility of understanding human existence'.[16]

The Protagonist in *Catastrophe* also reminds us of Beckett faced by the frightening notoriety that came with the Nobel Prize. A tantalizing biographical detail in the French text is the fact that the Protagonist's hands are clenched in Dupuytren's contraction, a condition Beckett suffers from. Moreover, when Suzanne Beckett learned that her husband had won the Nobel Prize for Literature, she whispered 'Quelle catastrophe' with a stricken look on her face.[17]

And let us not forget the theological level. That unseen Luke, in charge of lighting, may be the same evangelist who haunts *Godot*, Saint Luke who speaks of giving 'light to them that sit in darkness and in the shadow of death'. But what a light in *Catastrophe*!

In terms of classical mythology, the Protagonist is Promethean. He is a giver punished for giving to his people. And on the most universal level, *Catastrophe* delineates nothing less than the human plight. The Protagonist's suffering exemplifies that immemorial expiation to which all are condemned during *la catastrophe lente*, to use Henri Michaux's term, which is life itself.

Nevertheless, one overwhelming aspect of the great calamity of life is the endless series of catastrophes that humans wreck one upon the other in the name of governance or order, right, Reich, religion, progress or war; and the victims of these surgeons who operate with axes languish in hospitals, in cells, suffer observation, interrogations, violence. They undergo torture training in fields of mud, are warehoused in cylinders or cast out to wander as exiles. Their cries and their silences echo throughout not just *Catastrophe* but throughout Beckett's entire oeuvre. We are all prisoners, and to use

Beckett's two Greek titles, existence without eleutheria is catastrophe.

These social shadows, these historical and political resonances cannot be ignored. Literature is a social act and in A. A. Mendilow's words, 'even the most independent writer is grappled to the soul of his times with hoops of steel'.[18] To admit the social, political and historical is to grasp Beckett's works with more intensity, for in these realms his inexhaustible human compassion is most nobly visible.

Despite his sense of social responsibility, Beckett is far too pessimistic to believe in any theatre of political action or to hope for any general human emancipation. But through his writing he bears heroic witness to the grim facts of our existence and to all those protagonists who keep stubbornly going on. It is this tragic, caring awareness that is Beckett's glory.

Catastrophe is timeless while timely, specific while universal, artistically autonomous while politically committed. This outcry against forces both concrete and cosmic which strive to crush the human spirit is a distinguished addition to the canon of our preeminent living playwright.

THE *QUAD* PIECES: A SCREEN FOR THE UNSEEABLE

PHYLLIS CAREY

As Stanley Gontarski characterizes it, the final effect of the *Quad* pieces is 'one of prescribed, determined, enforced motion'.[1] Four players in long gowns and cowls pace an area in rhythmic movement, forming a quad shape with its diagonals and swerving to avoid the centre, termed in the script 'a danger zone'. The prescribed courses, exactness of the timing and the rhythmic, percussion accompaniment all produce an intricate ritual. But why are these robed creatures following the same repeated patterns? What is determining their movements? At least four overlapping levels of the ritual help one distinguish the determinate, the indeterminate, and the undeterminable in the dynamism of the *Quad* pieces. In these short mimes, Beckett weaves the mechanical, the mysterious, the mythic, and the television medium itself into an art work that inquires into the subtle interrelationship between making meaning and human being, between design and *Dasein*. All of which asks about *Sein*—Being—itself.

Perhaps the most apparent aspect of the *Quad* ritual is the machine-like quality of its rhythmic movement. The precision in movement and sound suggests both the Newtonian laws of motion and Descartes dream of an ideal machine that would run by itself. The rhythm suggests an intricate clock in which every movement is regulated. From this perspective, the human figures are subordinated to the pattern; they are cogs in a mechanism that—in the repetition of its movements—discloses an interminable, impersonal process.

The mechanism of movement suggests an underlying automatism, what Beckett calls in *Proust*, the 'automatic adjustment of the human organism to the conditions of its existence.'[2] But what is the source of the determinism in this mechanistic model? Is the automatism of *Quad* a statement about the author's understanding of reality or is it intended for interpreting existence? Like the lost ones whose environment depends on their perception,[3] the creatures of *Quad* both create and sustain the pattern, which in turn defines them. The dependence of the patterns on their human activators is stressed as much as the determinism of the courses once initiated. The mechanistic model of the universe derived from classical physics is inherently deterministic and entropic; furthermore, it has often been seen as reality itself rather than as a human concept for understanding reality. In its internal mechanism, *Quad* suggests both the determinism of the model and human complicity in bringing that model into existence and sustaining it through a blindness of its status as a rational concept—as merely one among many ways of interpreting reality.

If the mechanics of *Quad* suggest human adaptation to a deterministic, rational model, the mysterious centre, also created by the movements, draws attention to the limitations of rational knowledge. The designation in the television script of 'E' as 'supposed a danger zone'[4] and the deviations of the robed figures to avoid it disclose the dimension of the mysterious. While the mechanical appeals primarily to the rational, the mysterious appeals primarily to the imagination. The ritual of movement circumscribing patterns around an unknown centre implies a controlling fear, an erratic but rigid dance to appease the gods; the monk-like cowls and the repetition of processions constitute a wordless prayer. Like 'the ideal preying on one and all' in *The Lost Ones*,[5] which supposedly underlies the various rituals in that work, the centre of *Quad* suggests the mysterious realm of the unknowable, which determines the movement by the fear and homage paid to it. The existence and power of the unknown in determining the pattern, is, however, again dependent on the predispositions of the human figures. It is the 'supposing' of 'E' as a danger zone that creates and sustains it. Both reason and imagination create the figments that in turn become controlled determiners of human behaviour. The ritual of *Quad* dramatizes the rational and imaginative constructs humans have projected, which, in turn, have enslaved them.

In the staging of the human creation of the centre, *Quad* suggests a logocentrism that is tendential, projective, and imaginary. The centre that is present to the robed creatures as a projection of their fears is at the same time absent to the viewer. The transcendental signifier is, from different perspectives, both present and absent, affirmed and subverted. Yet such an approach to the mysterious centre of *Quad* does not completely account for its role within the ritual. Rather, its very indeterminacy—as something there and yet not there—shifts attention to the question of *Dasein*, the question of the 'being there' that inscribes it. It is the dread of the robed creatures that defines their design, that discloses their world as world. The nothingness at the centre of *Quad*, seen from this perspective, becomes a metaphor for that which cannot be determined. The undeterminable inner quad, that threatening central area, both underlies and pervades the temporal being there of the design.

Closely related to the realm of mystery in *Quad* are the mythical dimensions. The symbolic possibilities of the patterned movement take on an independence of the objects in which they are actualized. The emergence out of darkness and the return to darkness constitute an impersonal procession, analogous to a journey from birth to death. The Dantean overtones suggest the infernal agony of human existence. The figures in feverish monotony as though 'resisting a cold wind'[6] transcribe their patterns from initial darkness to final darkness. The cross-shape folding of their arms and the diagonal patterns within the quad that are doubled in the movements replicate the crucifixion, a recurring Beckettian motif. Human existence becomes the inscription of the anonymous, unchanging suffering of having been born. The determinism of this aspect of the dynamism flows from the womb-tomb darkness that precedes and follows the patterns. The unknowable origin and destiny make the procession an abandonment to the cross. Underlying the internal dynamism of the mechanical and partaking in the realm of the mysterious is the determinism of the indeterminable origin and destiny of the process, the inability to know the reason for it all that determines existence as an experience of Hell.

The aesthetic shaping of the *Quad* pieces, the fusion of the mechanical, the mysterious, and the mythical, suggests both a fascination with the intricacies of form and an attempt to reveal the formlessness behind the form. *Quad* constitutes a rhythmic dance that aspires to the status of temporal and spatial art. The intricacy and yet simplicity of the designs are aesthetically appealing both to the rational and the imaginative—'staging geometry' as Gontarski describes it.[7] There is delight in the permutation—like a kaleidoscope; like the sucking stones of Molloy, one is intrigued by the circulation and distribution. The mechanicality is aesthetically pleasing—like the symmetry that physics finds in the universe—in a leaf, in a snowflake. *Quad*, from the perspective of form does not need a determination of meaning, a controlling interpretation. Rather, like music and painting, it exists as a 'work' of art, purposive without purpose. Were that all, *Quad* could be seen primarily as an exercise in technique. Aesthetically, however, Beckett uses the television medium to interweave the various dynamisms into a meditation piece on the undeterminable.

Beckett's use of the mass media—as his use of language—consistently reveals the transparency of the medium. In another television play,

Eh Joe, Joe's face becomes the screen, while the Voice conjures the suicide of 'the green one'. The action takes place on an inner screen—the imagination—Joe's and the viewer's. Like the illusion of presence created by a pulsating beam of light moving rapidly across and down the face of a picture tube, the robed figures in *Quad* replicate the quadrangle of the television screen; the screen is made and unmade by the bent procession. Just as modern physics demands a recognition of the complicity between the observer and the observed, the television viewer is implicated in the process of *Quad*, creating with his/her perception the evanescent design the figures are tracing, increasingly aware that the design itself may be concealing what it would disclose. Like language in Beckett's drama, which often points beyond itself to the unsayable, the visual in *Quad* becomes a screen for the unseeable.

That Beckett intends the visual to serve as an enframing for the invisible is suggested by the very title of the play, 'Quad'. The words 'Quad' and 'Quadrat' recalls the white box of *Ping* and the four-square ruins of *Lessness* but also refer to the blank spaces between words, the blanking out mechanically between words in machine copy. The notion of 'Quad' as signifying the blank spaces between words underlines the importance of the spaces in the designs the figures inscribe. Ritual embodies the acting out of human signs. In the ritual of *Quad* the human figures define the spaces and particularly the inner quad that functions in the design, but the spaces in turn define the design. Like the spaces between words that separate groups of letters into signifying units and phrases, the spaces in *Quad* suggest *signi*ficant emptiness, analogous to the fullness of the pauses and silences in Beckett's spoken drama. The spaces, then, are as *sign*ificant visually as are the figures; without the spaces, there would be no design. Although the meaning of both space and figures may be ultimately indeterminate to the viewers, *Quad* would seem to point beyond that indeterminacy and the human preoccupation with determining to the undeterminable or what Heidegger calls the 'determinate, wholly indeterminate', the paradoxical nature of Being that is present in absence.[8] Like *Dasein* that *ex-ists*, that stands out from Being,[9] the figures and spaces that constitute the designs of *Quad* serve aesthetically as the ritualized embodiment of the question we as humans are. In his long excavation of language, Beckett leads us in the wordless mime of *Quad* to a silent contemplation of the enigma 'to be', without which there would be no design nor language at all.[10]

The *Quad* plays suggest the design-making of *Dasein* in all of its implications from ritual, to craftsmanship, to the inscribing of the signs of language, to the human need to de*sign*ate meaning. At the same time, these short mimes point beyond the configurations of *Dasein* to *Sein* itself, Being that determines but is itself indeterminate, whose ultimate mystery is humanly undeterminable. In the space between words, in the *quad* of the unseeable and the unsayable, Beckett leads us to a contemplation of Being whose expression we are. The purpose of *Quad* whether seen as a formalist exercise or a profound meditation on Being—may be simply to confound our will to determinism in its many manifestations, to lead us to a questioning and a 'letting be', to a readiness for the revelation of what is.[11] If, as Martin Heidegger suggests, knowing how to question means knowing 'how to wait, even a whole lifetime',[12] Samuel Beckett has shown us, simply and most profoundly, the design of that waiting.

NOTES

THE DIFFICULT BIRTH: AN IMAGE OF UTTERANCE IN BECKETT

Paul Lawley

1. Samuel Beckett, *The Complete Dramatic Works* (London: Faber, 1986) p 83.
2. Deirdre Bair, *Samuel Beckett: a Biography* (London: Jonathan Cape, 1978), pp 208-210.
3. 'Rehearsal notes for the German premiere of Beckett's *That Time* and *Footfalls* at the Schiller-Theater Werkstatt, Berlin (directed by Beckett)' trans. Helen Watanabe, *Journal of Beckett Studies* No 2 (Summer 1977), pp 83-95 (see esp pp 83-84).
4. The piece was first collected in Samuel Beckett, *Ends and Odds; Plays and Sketches* (London: Faber, 1977), pp 93-104 under the title *Radio II*, then in his *Collected Shorter Plays* (London: Faber, 1984), pp 113-124 under its definitive title *Rough for Radio II*. All references in the present study are to the text printed in *The Complete Dramatic Works* pp 273-284.
5. 'Beckett and the art of broadcasting' in Martin Esslin, *Mediations: Essays on Brecht, Beckett and the Media* (London: Methuen, 1980), p 149.
6. *Ibid.*, p 148.
7. For a comparable suggestion of male pregnancy see 'Afar a Bird' in Beckett, *Collected Shorter Prose* (London: John Calder, 1980), pp 195-196.
8. This passage seems to prefigure the episode with the hedgehog in *Company* (London: John Calder, 1980), pp 38-41.
9. In this passage 'living dead in the stones' seems to echo Lucky's 'abode of stones' in his 'Think' in *Waiting for Godot, Complete Dramatic Works*, p 42. The tunnels recall *Malone Dies*: 'Leaden light again, thick, eddying, riddled with little tunnels through to brightness, perhaps I should say air, sucking air. All is ready. Except me. I am being given, if I may venture the expression, birth to into death, such is my impression', Beckett, *Molloy, Malone Dies, The Unnamable* (London: Calder and Boyars, 1959), p 285. For critical comment see John Fletcher, 'Malone given "birth to into death"' in *Twentieth Century Interpretations of 'Molloy, Malone Dies, The Unnamable'*, ed. J.D. O'Hara (Englewood Cliffs, N J: Prentice Hall, 1970), pp 58-61.
10. *Complete Dramatic Works*, p 302.
11. Esslin, p 148.
12. *Pochade Radiophonique* has: 'une petite bête dans vos jolis dessous?' Beckett, *Pas, suivi de Quatre Esquisses* (Paris: Eds. de Minuit, 1978), p 66. The association with Fox—also a 'petite bête'—is clearer here. Also of note is the French version of Animator's comment on 'yesterday': '[I]t is down the hatch with love's young dream'—'il est tombé dans le trou avec les premiers baisers', *Pas*, p 83. The burrowing idea is present in 'dans le trou' and 'baisers' reappear in the phrase introduced by the Animator into Fox's utterance, 'entre deux baisers', *ibid*, p 85.

13 Beckett, *Proust and Three Dialogues with Georges Duthuit* (London: John Calder, 1965), p 124. Compare *Malone Dies*: 'Perhaps after all I am in a kind of vault and this space which I take to be the street in reality no more than a wide trench or ditch with other vaults opening upon it . . . Perhaps there are other vaults even deeper than mine, why not?', *Molloy*, etc p 219. And *The Unnamable*, where the pun is in sharper focus: 'Are there other pits, deeper down? To which one accedes by mine?', *Molloy*, etc p 295.
14 *Proust*, etc p 65.
15 *Ibid.*, p 64.
16 *Pochade Radiophonique* has: 'Si vous me rappeliez le passage, mademoiselle?' *Pas*, etc p 78; '[v]oulez-vous nous relire le passage, mademoiselle?' *ibid.*, p 84.
17 Compare Beckett's own comment on the dramatic situation in *Play:* 'The inquirer (light) begins to emerge as no less a victim of his enquiry than they (the figures in urns) and as needing to be free', letter to George Devine 'On *Play*' in Samuel Beckett, *Disjecta: Miscellaneous Writings and a Dramatic Fragment*, ed. Ruby Cohn (London: John Calder, 1983), p 112.
18 *Complete Dramatic Works*, pp 169-199. All my references are to the text printed in this edition.
19 *Beckett and Broadcasting: a Study of the Works of Samuel Beckett for and in Radio and Television* (Abo: Abo Akademi, 1976), p 39.
20 Letter to Nancy Cunard, 5 July 1956; quoted in Deirdre Bair, p 474.
21 *Samuel Beckett: a Critical Study*, new ed. (Berkeley, Ca.: U of California P., 1968), pp 169,170.
22 *Complete Dramatic Works*, p 166.
23 Charles R. Lyons, *Samuel Beckett* (London: Macmillan, 1983), p 89.
24 The best example comes after the taunting of the Rooneys by the Lynch twins. Dan muses: 'Did you ever wish to kill a child? (*Pause*) Nip some young doom in the bud. (*Pause*) Many a time at night, in winter, on the black road home, I nearly attacked the boy', p 191.
25 See note 5 above for full reference to *Malone Dies*.
26 *Complete Dramatic Works*, p 83.
27 The death of the little child is of course a recurring interpretative problem. My reading, as should be evident, is speculative and not exhaustive. The problem stems from the (very firm) suggestion that Dan is a murderer. It is in him and Maddy, as a couple, that the abhorrence of life conceived of as a process is confronted by horror at the event which is, it seems, the only termination of that process, death. Yet the taking of another life would distract, both morally and aesthetically, from this confrontation rather than clarify it. The identification Dan : Death :: Little Child : Maiden is attractive (and, I would guess, intended), but the mythopoeic personification of Dan still leaves him as a murderous *agent* on the literal, story level.
28 This paper could not have been completed without the help and encouragement of James Hansford and Vincent Mahon.
29 From *A Piece of Monologue*, *Complete Dramatic Works*, p 428.

LESS = MORE: DEVELOPING AMBIGUITY IN THE DRAFTS OF *COME AND GO*

Rosemary Pountey

1 Beckett's alterations to the manuscript are indicated by a line through the words (for his deletions); his second thoughts are shown in italics.
2 William Blake, *Songs of Innocence and of Experience* (London: OUP 1970), p 39.
3 *Oxford Book of German Verse from the 12th to the 20th Century*, ed. H.G. Fiedler (Oxford: OUP 1920), pp 77-78.

SEEING IS BELIEVING: BECKETT'S LATER PLAYS AND THE THEORY OF AUDIENCE RESPONSE

Karen L Laughlin

1 Extracts from Beckett's letters to Schneider on *Endgame* were published in *Village Voice* (19 March 1958), pp 8,15.
2 The term 'polyphonic' is borrowed from Paul Klee's discussion of artistic perception in his *The Thinking Eye* (London: Lund Humphries, 1961). See also Anton Ehrenzweig, *The Hidden Order of Art: a Study of Artistic Imagination* (Berkeley, Cal: U of California P., 1976), p 25.
3 The idea of 'laying bare' is taken from Shklovsky's remarks on 'defamiliarization' or 'the making strange' of familiar objects and techniques in order to promote our perception of them. See his 'Sterne's *Tristram Shandy*: stylistic commentary' in *Russian Formalist Criticism*, eds. Lee T. Lemon and Marion J. Reis (Lincoln, Nebr: U of Nebraska P., 1965), pp 25-57.
4 *Endgame* (New York: Grove P., 1958), p 81.
5 *Collected Shorter Plays* (New York: Grove P., 1984), p 157.
6 *Collected Shorter Plays*, p 301.
7 *Collected Shorter Plays*, p 241.
8 Keir Elam, *The Semiotics of Theatre and Drama* (London: Methuen, 1980), p 96.
9 Knowlson's observation that this gesture 'appears far more enigmatic in performance' than in the printed text—see James Knowlson and John Pilling, *Frescoes of the Skull: the later Prose and Drama of Samuel Beckett* (New York: Grove P., 1980), p 197—highlights the difference between a play's written text and the 'text' of its performance and hints at the problems involved in a discussion of spectator response based on the dramatic text. However Beckett's stage directions impose extreme limitations on productions of his plays, and this narrows a potentially wide gap. It produces what Alter calls a 'total text', the reading of which 'assumes that the play was written to be performed, and hence should be approached as a virtual performance, yielding an imaginary theatrical experience'. Such an approach certainly facilitates a study of play-audience interaction in Beckett's case.
10 *Collected Shorter Plays*, p 220.
11 This facet of Beckett's drama recalls Bachelard's comment that he did not like the theatre because you could not stop the action and the actors, as you could interrupt your reading, in order to dream.
12 *Collected Shorter Plays*, p 216.

13 Veltrusky, for example, defines drama as 'the literary genre rooted in dialogue'—see his *Drama as Literature* (Lisse: Peter de Ridder, 1977), p 48—while Serpieri notes that 'on stage *I* (in a dialectical relationship with *you*) prevails absolutely over the tertiary (and essentially narrative) *he*'. See Alessandro Serpieri (et al), 'Toward a segmentation of the dramatic text', *Poetics Today* 2, No 3 (1981), pp 163-200.
14 Serpieri, p 172.
15 Wolfgang Iser, *The Act of Reading: a Theory of Aesthetic Response* (Baltimore, Md: Johns Hopkins UP, 1978), pp 207-208.
16 Wolfgang Iser, 'The indeterminancy of the text: a critical reply', *Comparative Criticism: a Yearbook* 2 (1980), pp 27-47.
17 *Collected Shorter Plays*, p 215.
18 William B. Worthen, 'Beckett's actor', *Modern Drama* 24 (1983), pp 415-423.
19 Iser, 'The indeterminancy . . . ', p 35.
20 Enoch Brater, 'The "I" in Beckett's *Not I*', *Twentieth Century Literature* 20 (1974), pp 189-200.
21 Knowlson and Pilling, p 199.
22 Elam, p 96.
23 Anne Ubersfeld, *Lire le Theatre* (Paris: Eds Sociales, 1977), p 249.
24 *Collected Shorter Plays*, p 265.
25 *Ibid.*, p 265.
26 *Ibid.*, p 267, 269.
27 *Ibid.*, p 265.
28 Serpieri, p 178.
29 Elam, p 46.
30 *Collected Shorter Plays*, p 266.
31 Martin Esslin, 'A theatre of stasis: Beckett's late plays' in his *Mediations: Essays on Brecht, Beckett and the Media* (Baton Rouge, La: Louisiana State UP, 1980), pp 117-124.
32 Elam, pp 44-45.
33 Knowlson and Pilling, p 221.
34 Elam, p 56.
35 Iser, *The Act of Reading*, pp 96-101. See also his 'Interaction between text and reader' in *The Reader in the Text*, eds. Susan R. Suleiman and Inge Crossman (Princeton, NJ: Princeton UP., 1980), pp 106-119.
36 *Collected Shorter Plays*, p 240.
37 Knowlson and Pilling, p 222.
38 *Ibid.*, p 221.
39 Esslin, p 121.
40 *Collected Shorter Plays*, p 269.
41 *Ibid.*, p 242.
42 Ruby Cohn, 'Beckett's theatre resonance' in *Samuel Beckett: Humanistic Perspectives*, eds. Morris Beja, S.E. Gontarski, Pierre Astier (Columbus, Ohio: Ohio State UP, 1983), pp 3-15.
43 *Ibid.*, p 11.
44 Ehrenzweig (*cf* note 2), pp 22-25.
45 *Ibid.*, p 25.
46 *Ibid.*, p 26.
47 See, for example, the discussion of 'the geography of knowledge' in William E. Carlo, *Philosophy, Science and Knowledge* (Milwaukee, Wisc: Bruce, 1967), pp 6-19.
48 S.E. Gontarski, *The Intent of Undoing in Samuel Beckett's Dramatic Texts* (Bloomington, Ind: Indiana UP), 1985.

49 Ubersfeld, pp 39-40.
50 *Collected Shorter Plays*, p 316.
51 Antonin Artaud, *The Theatre and its Double*, trans. Mary Caroline Richards (New York: Grove P., 1958), p 38.
52 *Collected Shorter Plays*, p 154.
53 Una Chaudhari, 'The spectator in drama / drama in the spectator', *Modern Drama* 27 (1984), pp 281-298.
54 Shklovsky—*cf* note 3.

MUTATIONS OF THE SOLILOQUY: *NOT I* TO *ROCKABY*

Andrew Kennedy

1 I wish to apply one convenient (though arbitrary) distinction between 'monologue' as 'dramatic scene in which a single actor speaks' and 'soliloquy' as 'talking aloud to oneself'. The complexities of such a definition, found in *The Oxford Dictionary of English Etymology* (1966), are discussed by Raymond Williams in 'Talking to ourselves', *The Cambridge Review*, 27 April 1981, pp 160-164.
2 Terms used in Williams, p 162.
3 *Waiting for Godot* (London: Faber, 1965), pp 42-44. The rapid notation in the paragraph on Beckett's dialogue / monologue is fully discussed by me in the following: *Six Dramatists in Search of a Language* (London: CUP, 1975), pp 153-164; *Dramatic Dialogue* (London: CUP, 1983), pp 213-220; 'Krapp's dialogues of selves' in *Beckett at 80 / Beckett in Context*, ed. Enoch Brater (New York: OUP, 1986), pp 102-109; *Samuel Beckett: Form and Vision*—forthcoming.
4 See Keir Elam drawing on the work of Alessandro Serpieri in *The Semiotics of Theatre and Drama* (London: Methuen, 1980) and in '*Not I*: Beckett's Mouth and the Ars(e) Rhetorica' in *Beckett at 80 / Beckett in Context*, esp p 134. (I wrote this study before seeing Elam's article).
5 Public and private discussions with Roman Jakobson on the occasion of his visit to the University of Bergen.
6 R D Laing, *The Divided Self* (London: Tavistock, 1960), pp 129, 157.
7 Quoted from Mikhail Bakhtin, *Problems of Dostoevsky's Poetics*, ed. and trans. Carl Emerson (Minneapolis, Minn: U of Minnesota P., 1984) in Tzvetan Todorov, *Mikhail Bakhtin* (Manchester: Manchester UP, 1984). Todorov's context is here different: 'otherness and artistic creation'.
8 Beckett's own final note to *Not I* (London: Faber, 1973), p 16.
9 *Not I*, p 15.
10 Edith Oliver in *New Yorker*, 2 Dec 1972, quoted in *Samuel Beckett: the Critical Heritage*, eds. Lawrence Graver and Raymond Federman (London: Routledge and Kegan Paul, 1979), pp 328-329.
11 Hersh Zeifman, 'Being and non-being: Samuel Beckett's *Not I*', *Modern Drama* 19, No 1 (March 1976), pp 35-45.
12 James Knowlson and John Pilling, *Frescoes of the Skull: the later Prose and Drama of Samuel Beckett* (London: John Calder, 1979), p 219.
13 Andrew Kennedy, 'Krapp's dialogue of selves'—see note 3 above.
14 Kleist's essay 'On the Marionette theatre', and Beckett's interest in it, is discussed by Knowlson and Pilling, *op. cit.*
15 *Rockaby* in *Three Occasional Pieces* (London: Faber, 1982), p 25—my emphasis. My concluding reference is also to this section, pp 25-26.

ANONYMITY AND INDIVIDUATION: THE INTERRELATION OF TWO LINGUISTIC FUNCTIONS IN *NOT I* AND *ROCKABY*

Lois Oppenheim

1 Samuel Beckett, 'Dante . . . Bruno, Vico . . Joyce', *Transition* 16-17 (June 1929), p 242. Cited in Eugene F. Kaelin, *The Unhappy Consciousness* (Dordrecht: Reidel, 1981), p 15.
2 Keir Elam, '*Not I*: Beckett's Mouth and the Ars(e) Rhetorica' in *Beckett at 80 / Beckett in Context*, ed. Enoch Brater (New York: OUP, 1986), p 126.
3 *Ibid.*, p 127.
4 *Ibid.*, p 127.
5 *Ibid.*, p 128.
6 *Ibid.*, p 128.
7 Kaelin, *op cit.*, p 8.
8 *Ibid.*, p 302.
9 *Ibid.*, p 302.
10 (New York: St Martin's P., 1984).
11 *Ibid.*, pp 7-73.
12 Elam, p 126.
13 Samuel Beckett, *Not I* in *Collected Shorter Plays* (New York: Grove P., 1984), p 216.
14 Samuel Beckett, *Rockaby* in *Rockaby and Other Short Pieces* (New York: Grove P., 1981), p 9.
15 These oppositions are explored by Jacques Garelli in *Le Recel et la Dispersion* (Paris: Gallimard, 1978), p 15.
16 *Not I*, p 215.
17 James Knowlson and John Pilling, *Frescoes of the Skull: the later Prose and Drama of Samuel Beckett* (London: John Calder, 1979), p 199.
18 Enoch Brater, 'The "I" in Beckett's *Not I*', *Twentieth Century Literature* 20, No. 3 (July 1974), p 193.
19 Robert Champigny, 'Adventures of the First Person' in *Samuel Beckett Now*, ed. Melvin J. Friedman (Chicago: U of Chicago P., 1975), pp 119-128; cited in Elam, *op cit.*, p 135.
20 Butler, p 32.
21 *Rockaby*, p 20.
22 *Ibid.*, p 15.
23 Butler, p 8.
24 *Ibid.*, p 9.
25 *Ibid.*, p 9.
26 Jacques Garelli, *La Gravitation Poetique* (Paris: Mercure de France, 1966), p 9.
27 Brater, p 198.
28 *Not I*, p 218.
29 Samuel Beckett, *Breath* in *Collected Shorter Plays* (New York: Grove P., 1984), p 211.

WALKING AND ROCKING: RITUAL ACTS IN *FOOTFALLS* AND *ROCKABY*

Mary A. Doll

1 All references to these works will be from the following editions: *Footfalls* in *Ends and Odds: Eight New Dramatic Pieces* (New York: Grove P., 1976), pp 39-50; *Rockaby* in *Rockaby and Other Short Pieces* (New York: Grove P., 1981), pp 7-24.
2 Mircea Eliade, *The Sacred and the Profane: the Nature of Religion*, trans. Willard R. Trask (New York: Harper, 1959).
3 For an illuminating discussion of 'Orphic forces' that suggest strong connection with the myth of Orpheus in Beckett's early work, I am indebted to Peter Murphy, 'Orpheus returning: myth as "true story" in Samuel Beckett's *Still* trilogy', *International Fiction Review* 11, No 2 (Summer 1984), pp 109-112. See also Katherine Kelly, 'The Orphic Mouth in *Not I*', *Journal of Beckett Studies* 6 (Autumn 1980), pp 73-80. Both these articles cite Beckett's interest in Orphism, as evidenced by his signing of the document 'Poetry is Vertical' in *Transition: an International Workshop for Orphic Creation* 21 (March 1932), pp 148-149.
4 The Platonic pun reads, 'Our body is the tomb in which we are buried', (*Gorgias*, 493A). I am indebted to David L. Miller, Syracuse University, for help with references to Plato.
5 Murray Stein, *In Midlife: a Jungian Perspective* (Dallas: Spring Pubs., 1983), p 120. Other references to this work are cited by page number in my text.
6 Samuel Beckett, *Murphy* (New York: Grove P., 1957), p 107. Other references of mine to this work are from this edition.
7 Ritual means the giving of form or order. Words such as 'system', 'detailed method', 'procedure faithfully or regularly followed', suggest an interesting precision in the meaning of this word. See, eg, *The American Heritage Dictionary of the English Language*.
8 Mircea Eliade, *Cosmos and History: the Myth of the Eternal Return*, trans. Willard R. Trask (New York: Harper, 1959), pp 14, 12, 18.
9 To seek well is also to seek *by* the well, spring of self: to seek, in other words, for the source of one's own being. See Walter D. Asmus, 'Rehearsal notes for the German premiere of Beckett's *That Time* and *Footfalls* at the Schiller-Theater Werkstatt, Berlin (directed by Beckett)' trans. Helen Watanabe, *Journal of Beckett Studies* 2 (Summer 1977), pp 83-95.
10 *Plato's Phaedrus*, trans. R Hackforth (Cambridge: CUP 1952), 248B, p 79. Asmus, op cit., p 86, relates Beckett's comments on the nourishing role of words in the play. Beckett was taped as saying to the actress, 'You are looking for words which are "as food for the poor girl", you correct yourself constantly'.
11 Katherine H. Burkman, 'Initiation rites in Samuel Beckett's *Waiting for Godot*', *Papers in Comparative Studies* 3 (1984), p 141.
12 Deirdre Bair, *Samuel Beckett: a Biography* (New York: Harcourt, Brace, Jovanovich, 1978), p 382.
13 See my, 'The Demeter myth in Beckett', *Journal of Beckett Studies* – forthcoming.
14 Eliade, *Cosmos*, p 3.
15 Andrew Belis (pseudonym for Samuel Beckett), 'Recent Irish poetry', *The Bookman* 86 (August 1934), pp 235-236.
16 Samuel Beckett, *Proust* (New York: Grove P., 1957), p 11.
17 This idea is developed in Enrique Pardo, 'Dis-Membering Dionysus', *Spring* (1984), pp 163-179.

18 Suzanne Langer, *Feeling and Form* (New York: Scribner, 1953), p 50.
19 Samuel Beckett, *Company* (New York: Grove P., 1980).
20 Samuel Beckett, . . . *but the clouds* . . . in *Collected Shorter Plays* (New York: Grove P., 1984), pp 255-262. This television play, with its ellipsis in the title, expresses a deliberate spacing. In pronouncing the repeated key words, 'but the clouds', Beckett's actress also gives an elliptic effect, hauntingly. When her jaws drop at each vowel sound, it is hard to tell in the opening and closing whether her words are a blessing or a curse.

BECKETT'S OTHER TRILOGY: *NOT I*, *FOOTFALLS* AND *ROCKABY*

R Thomas Simone

1 Deirdre Bair, *Samuel Beckett: a Biography* (New York: Harcourt, Brace, Jovanovich, 1978), p 627. Bair's discussion of rehearsals for *Not I* continues on pp 628-630. It is best not to rely too heavily on Bair's biography since many questions have been raised about the reliability of its reporting. Ruby Cohn (see note 2) is far more reliable on such details.
2 *Just Play: Beckett's Theater* (Princeton, NJ: Princeton UP., 1980), pp 198-199.
3 James Knowlson, *'Happy Days': the Production Notebook of Samuel Beckett* (New York: Grove P., 1986), p 11.
4 The literature on Beckett's late plays is now beginning to expand. On all of Beckett's plays up to *A Piece of Monologue* (1979), see Ruby Cohn (note 2). On *Not I* see Hersh Zeifman, 'Being and non-being: Samuel Beckett's *Not I*', *Modern Drama* 19, No 1 (March 1976), pp 35-46. On *Footfalls*, see my '"Faint but by no means invisible": a commentary on Beckett's *Footfalls*', *Modern Drama* 26, No 4 (1983), pp 435-446, and Walter Asmus, 'Rehearsal notes for the German premiere of Beckett's *That Time* and *Footfalls* at the Schiller-Theater Werkstatt, Berlin (directed by Beckett)', trans Helen Watanabe, *Journal of Beckett Studies* 2 (Summer 1977), pp 83-95. Further rehearsal and production information will appear in Martha Fehsenfeld and Dougald McMillan, *Beckett at Work in the Theatre* (London: John Calder, forthcoming). See also Enoch Brater, *Beyond Minimalism: Beckett's Late Style in the Theatre* (New York: OUP, 1987).
5 Knowlson, p 22. These late plays refract, as Cohn suggests, images from the earlier works. I am thinking particularly of Winnie's hat in the 1979 *Happy Days* and the hat on the woman in the Buffalo and London premieres of *Rockaby*. See Cohn, pp 276-279, on the relation of the 1979 *Happy Days* to Beckett's earlier productions.
6 At the Beckett conference in Stirling Ruby Cohn expressed some doubts to me about whether Beckett had written all three of these plays 'for' Whitelaw. However Whitelaw herself in conversation at the conference explicitly said that Beckett had written *Footfalls* for her, and we know that Beckett wrote *Not I* specifically for her and was disappointed when the New York production of the play with Jessica Tandy preceded the Royal Court production with Whitelaw. The documentary film on the first production of *Rockaby* at Buffalo shows Whitelaw rehearsing the play with Alan Schneider and surely indicates that the play was written in response to Whitelaw as an actress. Thus, while respecting Cohn's authoriative views on Beckett, I believe that the assumption that Beckett has written a trilogy of plays for Whitelaw is a reasonable one.

7 'Visions of absence: Beckett's *Footfalls*, *Ghost Trio* and . . . *but the clouds* . . .' in *Transformations in Modern European Drama*, ed. Ian Donaldson (Atlantic Highlands, NJ: Humanities P., 1983), pp 121-122.
8 Quoted in Enoch Brater, 'Dada, Surrealism, and the genesis of *Not I*', *Modern Drama* 18, No 1 (March 1975), p 53.
9 Beckett's late plays exist in a number of editions. For convenience I cite all of these texts from Samuel Beckett, *Collected Shorter Plays* (New York: Grove P., 1984). Since the particular play is usually clear from the context of discussion, I cite only page numbers parenthetically from this edition.
10 *Happy Days* (New York: Grove P., 1961), p 7.
11 Cohn, p 213.
12 'Counterpoint, absence and the medium in Beckett's *Not I*', *Modern Drama* 26, No 4 (Dec 1983), p 412.
13 *Waiting for Godot* (New York: Grove P., 1954), p 58a.
14 Asmus, p 84.
15 Ned Chaillet, 'Beckett's *Rockaby*', *The Times* (London) 10 Dec 1982, p 11.
16 Asmus, p 83.
17 On a panel of actors and directors of Beckett with Walter Asmus and Pierre Chabert at the Stirling conference, Billie Whitelaw commented on her sense that Beckett approaches a play on stage as if it were sculpture. She told me that the picture of her as May in *Footfalls* is Beckett's favourite picture of her and that in it Whitelaw sees that sculptural expression. All members of that panel reinforced the idea that Beckett strives for a totally unified concept of drama that transcends the usual definitions of dramatic art. The terms used were most often drawn from the visual, musical and balletic arts than from the traditional vocabulary of drama.
18 Most of Beckett's directorial work in English has been recorded on video tape by the BBC. Perhaps the most influential television production, as mentioned in my essay, was Bill Morton's version of the 1973 Royal Court *Not I*, see Cohn, pp 213-215, and Esslin, pp 122-123. There is also a documentary film of the first production of *Rockaby* that was screened in Britain on the BBC in 1982 and in the United States on PBS in 1985. In addition there was a programme called 'Shadows' presented by the BBC that included *Not I*, . . . *but the clouds* . . . , and *Ghost Trio* that I have not yet seen. For those who have not seen any of these television versions some still photographs from the original productions can help in imagining the visual effect of these plays. The most impressive is probably the full page photograph of Billie Whitelaw as May in *Footfalls* in *At the Royal Court: 25 years of the English Stage Company*, ed. Richard Findlater (New York: Grove P., 1981), p 65 (cf note 17 above). On the facing page are photographs of Beckett rehearsing with Whitelaw in Act II of *Happy Days* and Brenda Bruce in Act I of that play (1962 production). In Charles R. Lyons, *Samuel Beckett* (New York: Grove P., 1983), p 105, we find an impressive photograph of her in the Buffalo, NY, premiere of *Rockaby*.

PERSPECTIVE IN *ROCKABY*

Jane Alison Hale

1 Published in English in *Rockaby and Other Short Pieces* (New York: Grove P., 1981), and in French in *Catastrophe et Autres Dramaticules* (Paris: Eds de Minuit, 1982). All further references to *Rockaby* and *Berceuse* will cite these editions.

2 'Light, sound, movement and action in Beckett's *Rockaby*', *Modern Drama* 25 (Sept 1982), p 345.
3 Charles Marowitz, 'Paris log', *Encore*, 9 (March – April 1962), p 44.
4 Telephone conversation with Ruby Cohn, as quoted in Ruby Cohn, *Just Play: Beckett's Theater* (Princeton, NJ: Princeton UP, 1980), p 31.
5 'Beckett piece by piece', *The Nation* 224 (19 Feb 1977), pp 217 – review of: Samuel Beckett, *Ends and Odds* (New York: Grove P., 1976); Samuel Beckett, *Fizzles* (New York: Grove P., 1976); Samuel Beckett, *I Can't Go On, I'll Go On; a Selection from Samuel Beckett's Works*, ed. and introduced by Richard W. Seaver (New York: Grove P., 1976); Steven J Rosen, *Samuel Beckett and the Pessimistic Tradition* (New Brunswick, NJ: Rutgers UP., 1976).
6 Cohn, p 31.
7 *Proust* (New York: Grove P., 1957), p 41.
8 Specified only in the later French version.
9 Cohn, p 35.
10 Cohn, pp 28,31.
11 Samuel Beckett, *More Pricks Than Kicks* (New York: Grove P., 1972), p 161.
12 Cohn, pp 71-72.
13 'An endless unveiling, veil after veil, plane after plane of imperfect transparencies, an unveiling towards the unrevealable, the nothing, the thing once more' (my translation) from 'Peintres de l'empêchement' in *L'Herne: Samuel Beckett*, eds. Tom Bishop and Raymond Federman (Paris: Eds de l'Herne, 1976), p 70.
14 See especially Beckett's opening remark on *Film* in *Film: Complete Scenario / Illustrations / Production Shots* (New York: Grove P., 1969), p 11.

KNOW HAPPINESS: IRONY IN *ILL SEEN ILL SAID*

Monique Nagem

1 Wallace Stevens, 'An ordinary evening in New Haven', in *The Palm at the End of the Mind* (New York: Vintage Books, 1972), pp 332-338.
2 Marjorie Perloff, 'Between verse and prose: Beckett and the new poetry', *Critical Inquiry* 9, No 2 (Dec 1982), pp 415-433.
3 Samuel Beckett, *Ill Seen Ill Said* (New York: Grove P., 1981), p 7. Subsequent references will be from this edition.
4 Perloff.
5 *Ibid.*
6 *Ibid.*
7 John Houston, *French Symbolism and the Modernist Movement: a Study of Poetic Structures* (Baton Rouge, La.: Louisiana State UP, 1980), pp 130-131.
8 Part of this undisclosed world, especially notable in Mallarmé's poetry, are the unconscious, hitherto repressed drives (*pulsions*) which Julia Kristéva discusses at length in *La Révolution du Langage Poétique* (Paris: Seuil, 1974), especially pp 209-262.
9 Quoted in Haraldo de Campos, 'Beyond exclusive language', in *Latin America in its Literature*, eds. C.F. Moreno and J. Ortega (New York: Holmes and Meier, 1980).
10 For a notable exception see Lawrence Harvey, *Samuel Beckett: Poet and Critic* (Princeton, NJ: Princeton UP, 1970).
11 Northrop Frye, *Anatomy of Criticism: Four Essays* (Princeton, NJ: Princeton UP, 1957), p 60.

12 Sharon Spencer, *Space, Time and Structure in the Modern Novel* (New York: New York UP, 1971), p 29.
13 Marjorie Perloff, 'Une voix pas la mienne. French / English Beckett and the French / English reader', unpublished paper delivered at the conference *Beckett Translating / Translating Beckett* at the University of Texas at Austin, March 1984.
14 Stéphane Mallarmé, *Oeuvres Complètes* (Paris: Gallimard, 1945), p 368.
15 Guy Delfel, *L'Esthétique de Stéphane Mallarmé* (Paris: Flammarion, 1951), p 98.
16 Mallarmé, p 442.
17 Gérard Genette, *Palimpsestes* (Paris: Seuil, 1982), introduction.
18 Frye, p 157.
19 Frye, p 160.
20 Frye, p 190.
21 Ludovic Janvier, *Beckett par Lui-Même* (Paris: Seuil, 1969), p 113.
22 Stevens, pp 331,333,335,349.
23 Alan Wilde, *Horizon of Assent: Modernism, Postmodernism and the Ironic Imagination* (Baltimore, Md: Johns Hopkins UP, 1981), p 1.
24 Quoted in Wilde, p 10.

READING *THAT TIME*

Antoni Libera

1 References are to the text as published in Samuel Beckett, *Collected Dramatic Works* (London: Faber, 1986), pp 385-395.
2 Samuel Beckett, *Disjecta: Miscellaneous Writings and a Dramatic Fragment*, ed. Ruby Cohn (London: John Calder, 1983), p 26.

THE SPEECH ACT IN BECKETT'S *OHIO IMPROMPTU*

Kathleen O'Gorman

1 Samuel Beckett, *Three Occasional Pieces* (London: Faber, 1982), p 30. References to *Ohio Impromptu* are to the text published in this edition.
2 *Ibid.*, p 30.
3 *Ibid.*, p 32.
4 *Ibid.*, p 31.
5 Yasumari Takahashi, 'Qu'est-ce qui arrive? Some structural comparisons of Beckett's plays' in *Samuel Beckett: Humanistic perspectives*, eds. Morris Beja, S.E. Gontarski, Pierre Astier (Columbus, Ohio: Ohio State UP, 1983), p 106.
6 *Ibid.*, p 106.
7 Henry Popkin, 'Beckett at 75', *The Listener*, 30 April 1981, p 590.
8 Charles R. Lyons, *Samuel Beckett* (London: Macmillan, 1983), pp 184-185.
9 Ruby Cohn, 'Beckett's theater of resonance' in *Samuel Beckett: Humanistic Perspectives* (cf note 5), p 14.
10 S.E. Gontarski, 'Review: the world premiere of *Ohio Impromptu*, directed by Alan Schneider at Columbus, Ohio', *Journal of Beckett Studies* 8 (Autumn 1982), p 133.
11 S.E. Gontarski, *The Intent of Undoing in Samuel Beckett's Dramatic Texts* (Bloomington, Ind.: Indiana UP, 1985), p 176.

12 *Ibid.*, p 176.
13 John L. Austin, *How to do things with words* (Cambridge, Mass: Harvard UP, 1962), p 3.
14 Keir Elam, *The Semiotics of Theatre and Drama* (New York: Methuen, 1983), p 158.
15 Austin, p 6.
16 *Ibid.*, p 150.
17 *Ibid.*, p 14.
18 *Ibid.*, p 108.
19 John Searle, *Speech Acts: an Essay in the Philosophy of Language* (Cambridge: CUP, 1969); see also his *Expression and Meaning: Studies in the Theory of Speech Acts* (Cambridge: CUP 1979).
20 Austin, p 52.
21 *Three Occasional Pieces*, p 30.
22 *Ibid.*, p 31.
23 *Ibid.*, p 29.
24 *Ibid.*, p 30.
25 S.E. Gontarski, *The Intent* . . . , p 176.
26 Cohn, p 14.
27 *Three Occasional Pieces*, p 32.
28 *Ibid.*, p 30 (line 34).
29 Jean – Francois Lyotard, *The Postmodern Condition: a Report on Knowledge*, trans. Geoff Bennington and Brian Massumi (Minneapolis, Minn.: U of Minnesota P., 1984), p 52.
30 *Three Occasional Pieces*, p 29.
31 See also Jan Mukarovsky, 'Poetic reference' in *Semiotics of Art: Prague School Contributions*, eds. Ladislav Matejka and Irwin R. Titunik (Cambridge, Mass.: MIT Press, 1976), pp 155-163; and Ladislav Matejka, 'Postscript: Prague School semiotics', *ibid.*, pp 265-290.
32 John R. Searle, *Expression and Meaning*, p 7.
33 As summarized in Elam, p 7.
34 Elam, p 88.
35 Mary Louise Pratt, *Towards a Speech Act Theory of Literary Discourse* (Bloomington, Ind.: Indiana UP, 1977), p 114.
36 Elam, p 170.
37 Elam, p 102.
38 Elam, p 164.
39 See Elam, p 95: 'A genuine phenomenology of audience competence founded on empirical research is an indispensable, though so far neglected, component of any theatrical poetics'.
40 *Three Occasional Pieces*, p 30.
41 *Ibid.*, p 30.
42 *Ibid.*, p 30.
43 *Ibid.*, p 29.
44 *Ibid.*, p 32.
45 S.E. Gontarski, *The Intent* . . . , p 177.
46 *Ibid.*, p 175.
47 *Three Occasional Pieces*, p 30.
48 S.E. Gontarski, *The Intent* . . . , p 177.

'MAKE SENSE WHO MAY': A STUDY OF *CATASTROPHE* AND *WHAT WHERE*

Annamaria Sportelli

1 Emile Benveniste, *Problèmes de linguistique générale*, vol 2 (Paris: Gallimard, 1980), p 220.
2 *Proust and Three Dialogues with Georges Duthuit* (London: John Calder, 1965), p 18.
3 *Ibid.*, p 11.
4 *Ibid.*, p 112. Quotation is from *Three Dialogues.*
5 *Ibid.*, p 13.
6 *Ibid.*, p 12.
7 *Ibid.*, p 19.
8 Benveniste, p 220.
9 René Thom, *Stabilité Structurelle et Morphogenèse* (Reading, Mass.: Benjamin, 1972).
10 René Thom, 'Logos – phénix', *Critique* No 387 (août-sept. 1979), p 799.
11 *Film* in *The Complete Dramatic Works* (London: Faber, 1986), p 323.
12 *Our Exagmination Round His Factification for Incamination of 'Work in Progress'* by Samuel Beckett (et al) (London: Faber, 1961), p 7.
13 *Complete Dramatic Works*, p 323.
14 *Ibid.*, p 87.
15 *Ibid.*, p 203.
16 *Ibid.*, p 307.
17 *Ibid.*, p 457.
18 *Ibid.*, p 457-458.
19 *Ibid.*, p 460.
20 Aristotle, *Poetics*, XI,10.
21 *Complete Dramatic Works*, p 461.
22 *Ibid.*, p 469.
23 *Ibid.*, p 470.
24 *Ibid.*, p 472.
25 *Ibid.*, p 476.

CATASTROPHE AND DRAMATIC SETTING

Hersh Zeifman

1 *En attendant Godot* (Paris: Eds de Minuit, 1952), pp 124-125.
2 *Endgame* (New York: Grove P., 1958), p 1. All further page references will be included in the body of my text.
3 Matthew 27:33.
4 Daniel 5:26, 30.
5 Edith Kern, 'Drama stripped for inaction: Beckett's *Godot*', *Yale French Studies* 14 (1954-55), pp 41-47.
6 See my article, 'Being and non – being: Samuel Beckett's *Not I*', *Modern Drama* 19, No 1 (March 1976), pp 35-46.
7 *Footfalls* in *Ends and Odds: Eight New Dramatic Pieces* (New York: Grove P., 1976), p 44. All further page references will be included in the body of my text.

8 *Footfalls* (London: Faber, 1976), p 11. Beckett's original manuscript of the play, and the five succeeding typescript versions, are in the Samuel Beckett Archive at Reading University Library (RUL MSS 1552/1-6).
9 T.S. Eliot, 'Burnt Norton' in *Four Quartets* (London: Faber, 1959), I, pp 14-15.
10 Walter D. Asmus, 'Rehearsal notes for the German premiere of Beckett's *That Time* and *Footfalls* at the Schiller Theater Werkstatt, Berlin (directed by Beckett)', trans. Helen Watanabe, *Journal of Beckett Studies* 2 (Summer 1977), pp 83-95.
11 *Murphy* (New York: Grove P., 1970), p 178.
12 See, for example: Martha Fehsenfeld, '*Catastrophe* (review of premiere)', *Theatre Journal* 35, No 1 (March 1983), pp 110-111; Rosette Lamont, 'New Beckett plays: a darkly brilliant evening', *Other Stages*, (16 June 1983), p 3; Edith Oliver, 'The theatre: off Broadway', *The New Yorker*, (27 June 1983), p 75; Mel Gussow, 'Beckett distils his vision', *The New York Times*, (31 July 1983), section H, p 3; Robert Brustein, 'Theater with a public dimension', *The New Republic*, (1 August 1983), pp 23-25; Antoni Libera, 'Beckett's *Catastrophe*', *Modern Drama* 28, No 3 (Sept 1985), pp 341-347.
13 *Catastrophe* in *Ohio Impromptu, Catastrophe* and *What Where: Three Plays* by Samuel Beckett (New York: Grove P., 1984), p 25. All further page references will be included in the body of my text.
14 See Lamont, *op. cit.*, p 3.
15 *Ibid.*, p 3.
16 *Waiting for Godot* (London: Faber, 1965), p 24.
17 In the Grove text, the word is misprinted as 'explication' (p 32). It is correctly printed as 'explicitation' in the original French text – *Catastrophe et Autres Dramaticules* (Paris: Eds de Minuit, 1982), p 77 – and in the first publication of the play in English – *The New Yorker*, (10 Jan 1983), p 26.
18 *The Shorter Oxford English Dictionary*, 3rd ed. with addenda (Oxford: Clarendon P., 1956).
19 See *Worstward Ho* (New York: Grove P., 1983), p 10.
20 Lamont, *op. cit.*, p 3.
21 See *Watt* (New York: Grove P., 1970), p 62.
22 *Proust and Three Dialogues with Georges Duthuit* (London: John Calder, 1965), p 125.
23 *Worstward Ho*, p 7.

A POLITICAL PERSPECTIVE ON *CATASTROPHE*

Robert Sandarg

1 S.E. Gontarski, *The Intent of Undoing in Samuel Beckett's Dramatic Texts* (Bloomington, Ind.: Indiana UP, 1985), p 80.
2 Samuel Beckett, *Collected Shorter Plays* (New York: Grove P., 1984), pp 312-313.
3 *Ibid.*, p 313.
4 Alfred Simon, *Beckett* (Paris: Belfond, 1983), p 42.
5 Diana Barth, 'Schneider directs Beckett', *Showbill* (Dec 1983), p 2.
6 Vivian Mercier, *Beckett / Beckett* (New York: Oxford UP, 1977), p 172.
7 Hugh Kenner, 'Samuel Beckett: putting language in its place', *New York Times Book Review*, (13 April 1986), p 35.
8 Barth, p 3.
9 Samuel Beckett, *Murphy* (New York: Grove P., 1961), p 187.

10 *Collected Shorter Plays*, p 299.
11 Samuel Beckett, *Catastrophe et Autres Dramaticules* (Paris: Eds de Minuit, 1982), p 73.
12 *Collected Shorter Plays*, p 297.
13 Mel Gussow, 'Beckett distills his vision', *The New York Times*, (31 July 1983), section H, p 3.
14 Samuel Beckett, *Malone Dies* (New York: Grove P., 1956), p 83.
15 Terry Eagleton, *Literary Theory* (Minneapolis, Minn.: University of Minnesota P., 1983), p 196.
16 Barth, p 3.
17 Deirdre Bair, *Samuel Beckett: a Biography* (New York: Harcourt Brace Jovanovich, 1978), p 604.
18 George Bluestone, *Novels into Film* (Berkeley, Cal.: University of California P., 1966), p 32.

THE *QUAD* PIECES: A SCREEN FOR THE UNSEEABLE

Phyllis Carey

1 S.E. Gontarski, 'Review: *Quad* I and II, Beckett's sinister mime[s]', *Journal of Beckett Studies* 9 (1984), p 137. Although the relationship between *Quad* I and II poses fascinating critical questions, my main purpose in this paper is to discuss the overall designs that characterize both versions of *Quad*.
2 *Proust* (New York: Grove P., 1970), p 9.
3 *The Lost Ones* (New York: Grove P., 1972), p 62.
4 *Quad* in Samuel Beckett, *Collected Shorter Plays* (New York: Grove P., 1984), p 293.
5 *The Lost Ones*, p 21.
6 Jim Lewis, quoted in Martha Fehsenfeld, 'Beckett's late works: an appraisal' in *Samuel Beckett: Modern Critical Views*, ed. Harold Bloom (New York: Chelsea House, 1985), p 225.
7 Gontarski, p 137.
8 Martin Heidegger, *An Introduction to Metaphysics*, trans. Ralph Manheim (New Haven: Yale UP, 1959), pp 78, 91. See also Lance St John Butler, *Samuel Beckett and the Meaning of Being: a Study in Ontological Parable* (London: Macmillan, 1984), pp 174-184.
9 Martin Heidegger, 'Vom Wesen der Wahrheit' in *Wegmarken* (Frankfurt a M.: Klostermann, 1967), p 86, cited in John Lascerbo, *Being and Technology: a Study in the Philosophy of Martin Heidegger* (The Hague: Martinus Nijhoff, 1981), p 189.
10 Heidegger, *An Introduction to Metaphysics*, p 72; see also Butler, p 178.
11 Heidegger, 'Vom Wesen der Wahrheit', p 189.
12 Heidegger, *An Introduction to Metaphysics*, p 206.

BIBLIOGRAPHY

The following general information is intended to supplement the detailed references found in the *Notes*.

1 *Works by Beckett*

The plays discussed in this book have been brought together in one-volume editions by publishers in the United States and Britain:

Samuel Beckett, *The Collected Shorter Plays* (New York: Grove Press, 1984).

Samuel Beckett, *The Complete Dramatic Works* (London: Faber, 1986).

Both these editions contain information on the dates of the first performances and publication of each play.

The prose work, *Ill Seen Ill Said*, is available also in American and British editions – by Grove Press, 1981 and by John Calder (London), 1982.

The standard bibliography of Beckett's writings is:

Raymond Federman and John Fletcher, *Samuel Beckett: his works and his critics* (Berkeley, Ca.: U. of California P., 1970). This has been supplemented by: Robin J. Davis, *Samuel Beckett: Checklist and Index of his Published Works 1967–1976* (Stirling: U. of Stirling, 1979); and

Breon Mitchell, 'A Beckett bibliography: new works, 1976–1982', *Modern Fiction Studies,* vol. 29 no. 1 (Spring 1983), pp. 131–152.

2 *Works on Beckett*

Federman and Fletcher (see above) covers only until the late sixties. The literature about Beckett's later writing is growing in volume but is not yet encapsulated within any one bibliography. If readers wish to supplement the reading suggested in the *Notes*, they must consult general reference works and databases.

NOTES ON THE CONTRIBUTORS

PHYLLIS CAREY, Assistant Professor of English, Marquette University, Wisconsin. Has written on Joyce and Beckett for the *James Joyce Quarterly*, and on the rituals of *Happy Days* in *Myth and Ritual in the Plays of Samuel Beckett*, ed. Katherine Burkman (forthcoming). Is preparing a full book-length study on Beckett.

MARY DOLL, Department of English, University of Redlands, California. Her publications have appeared in literary, psychological and educational journals. Is working on a book about Beckett and myth.

JANE HALE, Assistant Professor of Romance and Comparative Literature, Brandeis University, Massachusetts. Author of *The Broken Window: Beckett's Dramatic Perspective* (1987).

ANDREW KENNEDY, lectures in English at the University of Bergen, and is a Life Member of Clare Hall, Cambridge University. Has written *Six Dramatists in Search of a Language* (1975) and *Dramatic Dialogue: the Duologue of Personal Encounter* (1983) as well as numerous articles in literary and drama journals. Currently working on a monograph on Beckett.

KAREN LAUGHLIN, Associate Professor of English, Florida State University. Teaches courses in modern drama, play writing, contemporary literature and film, and has published articles on contemporary playwrights, dramatic theory and feminist theatre.

PAUL LAWLEY, Lecturer in English, Rolle College, Exmouth, Devon. Has published articles on Beckett in *Journal of Beckett Studies*, *Modern Drama* and *Modern Fiction Studies* and contributed essays on ten playwrights to *Contemporary Dramatists* (4th ed 1987).

ANTONI LIBERA, literary critic, translator, stage director, lives in Warsaw. Has translated all of Beckett's plays, and some of his other works, into Polish. Recently staged seven Beckett plays at the Warsaw 'Studio' theatre.

MONIQUE NAGEM, Assistant Professor of French and World Literature, McNeese State University, Louisiana. Translator of *Retable, La Reverie* by Chantal Chawaf (forthcoming).

KATHLEEN O'GORMAN, Assistant Professor of English, Illinois Wesleyan University. Has wide interests in modern British and Irish literature, and in modern American, British and European drama. Has published on Geoffrey Hill, James Joyce, Charles Tomlinson, and others.

LOIS OPPENHEIM, Assistant Professor of French, Caldwell College, New Jersey, and Acting Managing Editor of the *Journal of Philosophy*, Columbia University, New York. Author of *Intersubjectivity and Intentionality* (1980) – on Michel Butor, and numerous articles in literary and philosophical journals. Recently edited *Three Decades of the French New Novel*, and is currently working on a book on female characterization in Beckett and other contemporary writers.

ROSEMARY POUNTNEY, Jesus College, Oxford. Author of *Theatre of Shadows: from 'All that Fall' to 'Footfalls': Samuel Beckett's Drama 1956-76* (Irish Literary Studies, 28) (1988), and joint author with Nicholas Zurbrugg of the York Notes volume on *Waiting for Godot*. A professional actress, she has interpreted several of Beckett's roles.

ROBERT SANDARG, teaches French at the University of North Carolina, Charlotte. Has research interests in the contemporary French theatre, politics in literature, and Franco-American literary relations. Currently completing a book on Jean Genet and the Black Panthers.

TOM SIMONE, teaches Shakespeare and modern drama at the University of Vermont. Author of *Shakespeare's 'Lucrece'* (1976) and co-author of *Reclaiming the Humanities: the Roots of Self-Knowledge in the Greek and Biblical Worlds* (1986). Has published articles on Beckett, Pinter and Tolstoy and is currently working on a book on Ibsen and European nihilism.

ANNAMARIA SPORTELLI, university researcher, University of Bari. Has published essays on T.S. Eliot, T.E. Lawrence, and twentieth century Canadian literature. On Beckett, she has written on *Act without Words I and II*, *Film*, and *Play*, and is preparing a monograph study of his dramatic work.

HERSH ZEIFMAN, Assistant Professor of English, York University, Toronto, member of the editorial board of *Modern Drama* and of the executive board of the Samuel Beckett Society. Has written extensively on contemporary drama, especially the plays of Beckett, Pinter and Stoppard.

NOTES ON THE EDITORS

LANCE ST JOHN BUTLER, Lecturer in English Studies, University of Stirling, has just completed a year of teaching in France at the University of Pau. Author of *Samuel Beckett and the Meaning of Being: a Study in Ontological Parable* (1984). Has published on various aspects of English literature, and is known particularly for his work on Thomas Hardy – such as *Thomas Hardy after Fifty Years* (1977) and *Thomas Hardy* (1978).

ROBIN J. DAVIS, Associate Librarian, University of Stirling, and on the committee of *French XX Bibliography*. Has published a wide range of articles on librarianship and bibliography, and is particularly well known for his publications on Beckett, notably his *Essai de Bibliographie des Oeuvres de Samuel Beckett* (1971) and *Checklist of Samuel Beckett's Works 1967-76* (1979). A cousin of Samuel Beckett.

INDEX